We have reviewed the 2002 Probate Code.
Inside a Probate Sale: a Real Estate Agent's Guide
is still current, except some of the
California Association of Realtors
(CAR) forms and the local court rules.
February 9, 2002
Assistance Unlimited
Visit our website: www.probatesales.net

Inside a Probate Sale

A Real Estate Agent's Guide

By
Gayle Braswell Ellison
Probate Paralegal

Important: *Consult an attorney if questions occur. Changes in laws may render the information in this book invalid. Interpretations may differ; therefore, the author and publisher of this book make no guarantee as to its effectiveness. This book is intended for licensed real estate brokers or agents.*

Assistance Unlimited

Credits

Editor/Book Designer: Lura Dymond
Illustrator: Amanda Taylor
Legal Consultant: Virginia Palmer, Attorney at Law
　　　Fitzgerald, Abbott and Beardsley; Oakland, California

Important

Assistance Unlimited is committed to keeping this guide up-to-date. New editions will be printed from time to time to bring you current on any revisions in the law or minor changes in this guide. Assistance Unlimited will send you a notice when new editions become available.

Printed in the United States of America

Inside a Probate Sale:
A Real Estate Agent's Guide
© 1990 by Gayle Braswell Ellison
All Rights Reserved

ISBN 0-9624957-1-9
Library of Congress Catalog Card Number 89-85663
Assistance Unlimited
4480 Treat Boulevard, Suite 175
Concord, California 94521

Photo by Tustin Neil Ellison

About the Author

Gayle B. Ellison received her Probate Legal Assistant Specialist Certificate from California State University at Los Angeles in 1976. Since then she has devoted her efforts to perfecting her skills. For two years she was an in-house probate paralegal in Santa Ana, California, to attorney Ronald Prenner, who later became a Superior Court Judge in Orange County.

For the last twelve years she has been an independent, free-lance probate paralegal working for attorneys in Northern and Southern California. Recently she has changed her emphasis to consulting and writing in order to share her specialized knowledge with others.

Dedication

To my very best friend, Dee Sommars, for the suggestion that I write this guide; and

To my very dear husband, Tustin, for his never-ending support.

Acknowledgments

To Nell Fields, Marketing Director of the Daily Journal Corporation, Los Angeles, California, for her encouragement and support.

To Victoria Olson, author and teacher at Diablo Valley College in Pleasant Hill, California, for her assistance and suggestions.

To Rosie Frank, Larry Buster and Jack Corrigan of First American Title Insurance Company, Santa Ana, California, for their assistance.

To David H. Smith; Smith, Merrill, Mazer & Peffer; San Ramon, California, for his helpful advice.

To the Daily Journal Corporation for providing samples of legal advertising.

To the California Association of Realtors for permission to use some of their standard forms.

Table of Contents

Monterey County
Napa County
Nevada County
Orange County
Placer County
Plumas County
Riverside County
Sacramento County
San Benito County
San Bernardino County
San Diego County
San Francisco County
San Joaquin County
San Luis Obispo County
San Mateo County
Santa Barbara County
Santa Clara County
Santa Cruz County
Shasta County
Sierra County
Siskiyou County
Solano County
Sonoma County
Stanislaus County
Sutter County
Tehama County
Trinity County
Tulare County
Tuolumne County
Ventura County
Yolo County
Yuba County

Sample Forms Included in This Guide

Introduction

The name of the game is to close a real estate sale fast and get the commission in your pocket. This guide will provide you with the knowledge to close a probate sale faster and with less hassle. You can astound your client, your broker, and the escrow company with your professionalism and outstanding service, not to mention the fact that closing the sale faster will free up your time to generate other sales.

How would you like to hear your client say, "You're the best thing that has ever happened to me!"? The "nuts and bolts" guidelines set out in this book will give you the information necessary to impress your client and get such a favorable reaction.

The interaction and cooperation between you, your client, the estate representative, and the attorney in a probate sale are of greater importance than ever before.

In the past the court played a major and active role in the administration of an estate in that almost every act required court approval. The numerous hearings to obtain such approval resulted in the court's calendar being overcrowded. Once the representative made a decision to sell, a delay was usually experienced while the attorney prepared the papers and applied for a hearing date. In many instances the hearing date was continued because the paperwork presented to the court was *incorrect because the sale procedures were not performed in the correct manner*, resulting in needless delay and expense. This scenario is still often the case today.

However, on July 1, 1988, the New Supervised Administration of Decedent's Estates went into effect, adopting a uniform set of procedures, aimed at simplifying the administration of an estate.

The purpose of the new legislation and revisions made in the Probate Code in the last several years is to allow the estate representative—the executor, administrator, guardian or conservator—to administer portions of the estate without direct court supervision by establishing guidelines that the representative can follow. If the representative stays within the guidelines for sales, no personal liability is likely to occur and a court hearing will not be necessary. However, to avoid liability, it will be of greater importance than ever before that the representative follow the court-enacted guidelines, and that the attorney and the real estate broker help monitor the process.

If your client is the personal representative of the estate, he or she probably will not know about sale matters and will be relying upon his or her attorney for legal guidance. Your knowledge of some of these procedures will ease the relationship with your client and the client's attorney, resulting in the sale being handled in a more expedient manner.

Using this guide as a quick and easy reference will result in fewer headaches and aggravation when you list a piece of probate property for sale.

If your client is not the estate representative, but someone who is interested in buying a piece of probate property, then you need to be knowledgeable about the procedure so that you will be able to properly advise him or her. You want to know what you are doing when you go into court to bid if the sale requires court approval, or when negotiating with the representative if it does not.

Once you understand probate sales, you will readily see that they are not anything to be afraid of. Indeed, they are a handy way to increase your list of both clients and properties, and boost your sales.

Chapter 1

Who, What and When: Definitions

 How does a piece of property become part of an estate and be sold in a probate sale? Who are the people you will be meeting during the process?

In order for you to talk more knowledgeably with those persons involved, it will be helpful to review some basic terms and their meanings.

The property you will be helping to sell, or assisting clients to purchase, is under the jurisdiction of the probate court and is governed by the California Probate Code. You are probably most familiar with probate and have a general idea of what it does, but such property can also be in a conservatorship, guardianship, or trust.

Personal Representative

The person who is administering the property, and with whom you will be dealing, is called the personal representative. This person may be an executor, administrator, guardian, conservator or trustee. Each of these representatives is appointed by the court. The representative may be your client, as the seller. Or you may be representing the potential buyer of the piece of probate property.

Probate

As you know, probate takes place when a person dies. It is not always necessary to have a probate occur — property can be transferred by joint tenancy or as community property, for instance. The deceased person in a probate is called a decedent in legal jargon. The process involves having a personal representative appointed, settling the claims of creditors, inventorying the estate, paying any taxes due, administering the estate during probate, and then distributing the estate to the appropriate heirs or beneficiaries.

Executor.

The executor is the person named in a decedent's Will to administer the estate.

Administrator.

The administrator is appointed by the court to administer the estate when the decedent did not leave a Will (called **dying intestate**).

Administrator With Will Annexed.

The administrator with the Will annexed is the person or fiduciary appointed by the court to administer the estate when the decedent left a Will but did not name an executor, or an executor was named but does not act and no alternate executor was named.

Special Administrator.

A special administrator is appointed to serve in an interim capacity when there are matters needing immediate attention, such as an ongoing business.

Interested Persons.

Interested persons are persons who are named in the Will as beneficiaries or who will inherit property pursuant to the law of intestate succession because the decedent did not leave a Will, or because the Will did not transfer all of the property of the decedent. Interested persons may also be creditors of the decedent.

Guardianship

Guardian.

A guardian is appointed by the court to take care of the person and/or the estate of a child under the age of 18. There can be two guardians, one for the person and one for the property, or one person can do both jobs.

Conservatorship

Conservator.

A conservator is appointed by the court to take care of the person and/or estate of an individual, over the age of 18, who is incapable of managing either his or her own personal needs for food, clothing and medical care; or his or her own financial affairs. Again, this may be two separate persons, or one — or it may be an institution.

Limited Conservator.

A "limited" conservatorship may be established for a developmentally disabled adult. The powers of the conservator in this instance are limited to promoting and protecting the well-being of the disabled person, allowing the disabled person to be as independent and self-reliant as the circumstances permit.

Trust

Trustee.

A trustee manages the property of a trust. There are two kinds of trusts: a testamentary trust or a living trust (also known as an inter vivos trust). A testamentary trust is established in a Will and takes effect after the individual's death. The trustee is appointed by the court.

A living (inter vivos) trust is set up while the person is still alive; the individual transfers his or her property to the trust. The trustee of a living (inter vivos) trust is named in the trust and is not court-appointed; often it is the person who formerly owned the property and who still manages it as trustee.

Notice vs. Consent

Most probate petitions require that a written notice of the hearing of the petition be sent via the mail to the heirs or beneficiaries and other interested persons. The notice period in most instances is 15 days.

In some situations, the probate court will approve a petition if the interested and affected persons sign a consent, consenting to the action requested in the petition. See Form 4, Notice of Proposed Action re Intent to List Property, for an example where the consent procedure is appropriate.

Reasons for Selling Property

There are several reasons why a personal representative may find it necessary to sell real property in an estate:

- To pay debts, bequests, family allowance, expenses of administration or taxes.
- The Will directs the property be sold.

- The property is a financial drain on the estate.
- Character of the property (not easily distributed to more than one person).
- Condition of the market for selling the property.
- Dissension among the heirs.

The personal representative needs expert advice to make sure that all the legal requirements of the Probate Code are met; for this, he or she relies on the attorney representing the estate. You will also be dealing with the attorney and relying on his or her specialized knowledge.

But the personal representative also needs an expert in the field of real estate, who can see that the top price with the most benefit to the estate is received, and that the sale is handled efficiently and quickly. This is where you come in. In this regard, you're a very valuable member of the team.

NOTES

Chapter 2

Independent Administration of Estates Act

 The Independent Administration of Estates Act (IAEA) was enacted to allow personal representatives of probate estates to handle appropriate routine actions, such as sales of real and personal property, without court approval. On July 1, 1988, a new part of the act became operative, which gives the representative more authority to function without court supervision. (Probate Code Section 10400 and following.) The authority to so act must be granted by the court, usually when the representative is appointed.

Guardianships, conservatorships and trusts are not administered under the IAEA.

Before you proceed with a sale transaction, inquire of the representative's attorney if the sale will be conducted under the Independent Administration of Estates Act. If so, then the following will be beneficial so that you will understand the procedures in an IAEA sale.

You should be aware that the Will may restrict the powers of the personal representative so that IAEA powers cannot be used.

When authority is granted to the personal representative to administer the estate under the IAEA, the court specifies whether the powers granted are full or limited.

Full IAEA Powers

When the personal representative has *full* powers and sells property under the IAEA (Probate Code Section 10503), the sale may be:

- At either public auction or private sale;
- With or without notice;
- For such price;
- For cash or on credit; and
- Upon such terms and conditions as the personal representative may determine.

A real estate sale in this situation will proceed much like a regular sale. The personal representative will negotiate the price and terms of the sale much as any other seller would do. You and the potential buyers will be aware that this is a probate sale and that fact will be evident in escrow, but the requirements for court supervision detailed in the following chapters of this book will not apply.

However, even if the personal representative has *full* powers, he or she and the attorney for the estate may decide to ask for court confirmation of the sale. They may feel that this will help them obtain more potential buyers and a better price during the overbidding process, or they may want to be sure that the personal representative does not incur any liability in the sale. You need to have a clear understanding of how the representative and the attorney wish to handle the sale.

Limited IAEA Powers

Real estate transactions are the one area that has been specifically deleted from IAEA powers when the representative has only *limited* powers (Probate Code Section 10501).

A personal representative with only *limited* authority must obtain court approval for the following actions:

- Sell real property;
- Exchange real property;
- Grant an option to purchase real property;

- Borrow money with the loan secured by an encumbrance on real property.

For your purposes, then, handling a sale when the representative has *limited* powers will be like a sale when the representative does *not* have IAEA powers. The necessary steps to acquire court approval of the sale will have to be followed, as detailed in the next few chapters of this book. They include, briefly, publication of the notice of sale; court approval of the sale and commissions; the sale to be at not less than 90% of appraised value; and the court's examination into the necessity of the sale, the advantage to the estate, and the efforts to obtain the highest and best price. (What constitutes a sale for 90% of the appraised value varies from county to county. Check the local court rules in the appendix.)

When Selling to the Personal Representative or the Attorney

Even with full powers under IAEA, court approval must be obtained (Probate Code Section 10501) *when*:

- Estate real property is sold to the personal representative or to the attorney for the personal representative.

- Estate real property is exchanged for property of the personal representative or for property of the attorney for the personal representative.

- An option is granted to purchase property of the estate to the personal representative or to the attorney for the personal representative.

There is an exception to this requirement if the personal representative is the sole beneficiary of the estate or all the known heirs or beneficiaries have consented to the sale. Also, the period for creditors to submit claims must have expired and all the claims have been settled or the creditors must have consented. In addition, all those requesting special notice, if any, must have consented.

If you are involved in a situation of this type, discuss it with the personal representative and the attorney to determine whether the powers granted under the IAEA may still be useful.

Notice of Proposed Action

A notice of proposed action must be given on certain occasions. The notice must be in writing and sent to the interested persons, i.e., heirs at law, beneficiaries under the Will, and anyone who has requested special notice of the probate proceeding. The notice must be mailed 15 days prior to the date the proposed action will be taken. If objections to the proposed action are made during the 15-day period, then a court order is required to proceed with the action.

Actions Which Require Notice.

The actions concerning real or personal property sales where the personal representative must give notice are as follows:

1. Selling or exchanging personal property. (Probate Code Section 10537.)

2. Selling or exchanging real property. (*Limitation*: the personal representative must have *full* IAEA powers or the court must approve the act.) (Probate Code Section 10511.) See Form 1.

3. Abandoning tangible personal property when the cost of collecting, maintaining, and safeguarding the property would exceed its fair market value. (Probate Code Section 10513.)

4. Borrowing, placing, replacing, renewing, or extending any encumbrance upon any property of the estate. (*Limitation*: only a personal representative with *full* authority can borrow money with the loan secured by an encumbrance on real property; otherwise, court approval must be obtained.) (Probate Code Section 10514.)

5. Granting an option to purchase real property of the estate during or beyond the period of administration. (*Limitation*: the personal representative must have *full* IAEA powers or the court must approve the act.) (Probate Code Section 10515.)

6. Entering into a contract where the contract is not fully performed within two years. (*Exception*: if the personal representative has the power to terminate the contract within two

years, no notice is necessary.) (Probate Code Section 10532.)

7. Entering as lessor into a lease of real or personal property for more than one year and/or giving the lessee the right to extend the term of the lease. The period, terms and conditions are at the discretion of the personal representative. (Probate Code Section 10536.)

Actions Which Do Not Require Notice.

The personal representative may take the following actions without giving notice of proposed action:

1. Generally manage and control estate property. (Probate Code Section 10531.)

2. Enter into a contract in order to carry out a specific power bestowed under the IAEA. (*Exception*: if the contract will not be fully performed within two years, notice must be given.) (Probate Code Section 10532.)

3. Enter as lessor into a lease of personal or real property for less than one year. The period, terms and conditions are at the discretion of the personal representative. (*Exception*: notice must be given if the lease gives the lessee the right to extend the term of the lease.) (Probate Code Section 10536.)

4. Make repairs and improvements to real and personal property of the estate. (Probate Code Section 10562.)

5. Pay taxes and assessments and expenses incurred in the collection, care, and administration of the estate property.

6. Accept a deed to property which is subject to a mortgage or deed of trust in lieu of foreclosure of the mortgage or sale under the deed of trust. (Probate Code Section 10563.)

7. Give a partial satisfaction of a mortgage or cause a partial reconveyance to be executed by a trustee under a deed of trust held by the estate. (Probate Code Section 10564.)

An Exclusive Right to Sell Contract.

Since an exclusive right to sell contract is important to you and your pocketbook, let's take a moment to examine how it is treated under the IAEA.

Certain transactions can be performed by the personal representative having *full* authority *without* giving a Notice of Proposed Action:

- Granting an exclusive right to sell property contract for a period not to exceed 90 days.

- Granting to the same broker one or more extensions of an exclusive right to sell property contract, each extension being for a period not to exceed 90 days.

However, if the original exclusive right to sell and all extensions total more than 270 days, the personal representative must give a Notice of Proposed Action (Probate Code Section 10538).

If the exclusive right to sell contract has been renewed more than twice, contact the attorney for the representative to make sure the proper Notice of Proposed Action has been given. The notice routine takes a minimum of 15 days. To save time, the notice to the interested persons can be waived. Ask the representative's attorney if a waiver of notice of proposed action is possible.

As we'll discuss more fully in the next chapter, the listing broker is not assured a commission unless the listing is exclusive.

Use of IAEA Where All Beneficiaries Consented

Background:

A husband and wife lived in two separate residences. The title to both properties was held in joint tenancy by the husband and his wife (it was also community property). As you know, when one joint tenant dies, the property automatically passes to the surviving joint tenant.

On his death bed, the husband executed deeds for his one-half interest in the houses from himself as a joint tenant to himself as a tenant in common. Because it was still community property, his wife was entitled to her one-half interest, but would no longer be certain to receive her husband's half interest as she would have under joint tenancy. In his Will the husband excluded his wife and gave his one-half community property in equal shares to his five sons.

To accommodate distribution and to pay expenses of administration, it was necessary to sell the house in which the husband had lived. The decedent owned one-half of the house and his surviving spouse owned the other one-half, so it was necessary to obtain the consent of the surviving spouse. She, of course, was angry because her husband had deprived her of inheriting his half interest.

Procedure:

The husband's brother, who lived on the East Coast, was appointed executor. He signed an exclusive listing agree-

ment using his *IAEA* powers. *All documents were sent to him by Federal Express to prevent delay.*

Immediately after the appointment of the representative, the attorney set in motion the procedures to have the house appraised by the probate referee.

Within 20 days after the executor was appointed, an offer to buy the property was received.

The attorney sent a Notice of Proposed Action to the surviving spouse and the five sons, stating that on or after 15 days the executor would open an escrow. They each signed the consent on the back of the notice and returned it to the executor's attorney. Since the signed consents showed that the surviving spouse and the sons were in agreement, the escrow was opened 16 days after the notice was sent.

Because all beneficiaries and the surviving spouse consented to the sale and because the property sold for more than the appraised value, the representative would incur no personal liability as to the sale or selling price. Therefore, court confirmation was not necessary.

Sequence of Events:

The representative was appointed on November 8.
The property was listed on November 9.
The court appraisal was completed on December 22.
The notice was sent on December 8, stating that the escrow would close on or after January 7.
The escrow closed on January 26 and the real estate agent received a commission.
Seventy-eight days elapsed from the time the property was listed to the close of escrow.

Moral of the Story:

This could have been a difficult probate sale, but instead it was handled orderly and efficiently.
Two factors could have delayed this sale:

- *The attitude of the surviving spouse, who was angry because her husband left his one-half of their community property to his sons instead of to her. However, due to the smooth handling of the attorney and executor, she acquiesced to the terms of her husband's Will, and the sale proceeded timely.*

- *The distance of the representative. The attorney for the representative played an active role, since the executor lived out of state. All documents requiring the executor's signature were sent to him by Federal Express, preventing any delay due to distance.*

It just takes knowing the procedures and communicating with the representative, all interested parties and the attorney.

ATTORNEY OR PARTY WITHOUT ATTORNEY *(Name and Address):*
JOHN Q. LAWYER
100 City Justice Building
Suite 200
Heavenly, CA 90000
TELEPHONE NO.: (415) 100-1000
ATTORNEY FOR *(Name):* Petitioner

FOR COURT USE ONLY

SUPERIOR COURT OF CALIFORNIA, COUNTY OF COMFORT
STREET ADDRESS: Court Building
MAILING ADDRESS: Court Building
CITY AND ZIP CODE: Heavenly, CA 900000
BRANCH NAME:

ESTATE OF (NAME): N. O. LONGERHERE

DECEDENT

NOTICE OF PROPOSED ACTION
Independent Administration of Estates Act
Objection – Consent

CASE NUMBER:
10000

NOTICE: If you do not object in writing or obtain a court order preventing the action proposed below, you will be treated as if you consented to the proposed action and you may not object after the proposed action has been taken. If you object, the personal representative may take the proposed action only under court supervision. An objection form is on the reverse. If you wish to object, you may use the form or prepare your own written objection.

1. The personal representative (executor or administrator) of the estate of the deceased is *(names):*
I. M. STANDIN

2. The personal representative has authority to administer the estate without court supervision under the Independent Administration of Estates Act (Probate Code section 10400 et seq.)
   a. ☒ with full authority under the act.
   b. ☐ with limited authority under the act (there is no authority, without court supervision, to (1) sell or exchange real property or (2) grant an option to purchase real property or (3) borrow money with the loan secured by an encumbrance upon real property)

3. On or after *(date):* _____ , the personal representative will take the following action without court supervision *(describe in specific terms here or in Attachment 3):*
   ☐ The proposed action is described in an attachment labeled Attachment 3.
Sell the real property located at 10 Best Place, City of Heavenly, County of Comfort, State of California, to Bill and Betty Buyer, for the sum of $200,000, on the terms and conditions set forth in the Real Estate Purchase Contract and Receipt for Deposit attached here-to as Exhibit A and made a part hereof by reference. The sale is subject to and conditioned upon either notice of sale being given pursuant to Section 10580 of the Probate Code and no objection or revocation of consent being received; or all required consents being received pursuant to Section 10582 of the Probate Code.

4. ☒ Real property transaction *(Check this box and complete item 4b if the proposed action involves a sale or exchange or a grant of an option to purchase real property.)*
   a. The material terms of the transaction are specified in item 3, including any sale price and the amount of or method of calculating any commission or compensation to an agent or broker.
   b. $ 200,000 _____ is the value of the subject property in the probate inventory. ☐ No inventory yet.

NOTICE: A sale of real property without court supervision means that the sale will NOT be presented to the court for confirmation at a hearing at which higher bids for the property may be presented and the property sold to the highest bidder.

(Continued on reverse)

Form Approved by the
Judicial Council of California
DE-165 (Rev. July 1, 1988)

NOTICE OF PROPOSED ACTION
Objection – Consent
(Probate)

Probate Code, § 10580 et seq.

Form 1, Page 1

ESTATE OF (NAME): N. O. LONGERHERE		CASE NUMBER:
	DECEDENT	10000

5. If you OBJECT to the proposed action
   a. Sign the objection form below and deliver or mail it to the personal representative at the following address *(specify name and address)*: John Q. Lawyer
      100 City Justice Building, Suite 200
      Heavenly, CA 90000

   – OR –
   b. Send your own written objection to the address in item 5a. *(Be sure to identify the proposed action and state that you object to it.)*

   – OR –
   c. Apply to the court for an order preventing the personal representative from taking the proposed action without court supervision.

   d. **NOTE:** Your written objection or the court order must be received by the personal representative before the date in the box in item 3, or before the proposed action is taken, whichever is later. If you object, the personal representative may take the proposed action only under court supervision.

6. If you APPROVE the proposed action, you may sign the consent form below and return it to the address in item 5a. If you do not object in writing or obtain a court order, you will be treated as if you consented to the proposed action.

7. If you need more INFORMATION, call *(name):* John Q. Lawyer
   (telephone): (415) 100-1000

Date:

. . . . ▶ _____
(TYPE OR PRINT NAME)   (SIGNATURE OF PERSONAL REPRESENTATIVE OR ATTORNEY)

OBJECTION TO PROPOSED ACTION

☐ I OBJECT to the action proposed above in item 3.

NOTICE: Sign and return this form (both sides) to the address in item 5a. The form must be received before the date in the box in item 3, or before the proposed action is taken, whichever is later. *(You may want to use certified mail, with return receipt requested. Make a copy of this form for your records.)*

Date:

. . . . ▶ _____
(TYPE OR PRINT NAME)   (SIGNATURE OF OBJECTOR)

CONSENT TO PROPOSED ACTION

☐ I CONSENT to the action proposed above in item 3.

NOTICE: You may indicate your **consent** by signing and returning this form (both sides) to the address in item 5a. If you do not object in writing or obtain a court order, you will be treated as if you consented to the proposed action.

Date:

. . . . ▶ _____
(TYPE OR PRINT NAME)   (SIGNATURE OF CONSENTER)

DE-165 [Rev. July 1, 1988]   NOTICE OF PROPOSED ACTION   Page two
                                   Objection – Consent
                                      (Probate)

Form 1, Page 2

NOTES

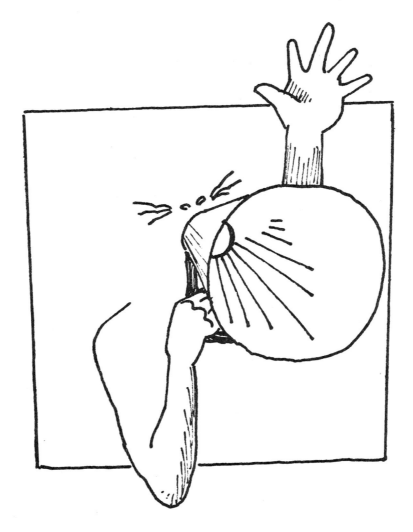

"Call the attorney for the estate."

Chapter 3

Prior to Signing the Listing Agreement

 There are a number of legal procedures which the attorney must deal with before you actually ask your seller to sign the listing agreement. If these procedures have not been considered or completed, the sale may not be legally valid and the sale procedure might have to be started all over again. The ineptness, delay and confusion could cause you to lose a buyer, not to mention the frustration everyone concerned will experience.

Contact the Attorney

As soon as the seller tells you that you will be handling the sale *and before the listing agreement is signed,* contact the attorney who is handling the probate to make sure the necessary procedures have been taken care of prior to the property actually being listed. You should discuss with the attorney the following:

Is There a Power of Sale in the Will?

Does the Will contain a power of sale clause regarding the sale?

A typical power of sale clause in a Will might read as follows:

"**I authorize my Executor to sell,** assign, transfer, encumber, hypothecate, or otherwise alienate, including the right to rent, lease or bail with or without notice, **at either public or private sale, any property, real,** personal or mixed, tangible or intangible, or any interest therein, **belonging to my estate, subject to such confirmation of court as may be required by law.**"

If the Will does not contain a power of sale clause, then a Notice of Sale of Real Property at Private Sale must be published. (See Form 2 at the end of this chapter.) The notice is published in a local newspaper and basically says that on or after a certain date the property will be sold to the highest bidder. The notice also contains the terms of sale. You can list the property before the notice has been published, but if you obtain a buyer, *the property cannot be legally sold until after the date stated in the notice*. The attorney will handle this notice procedure, which will take approximately three weeks.

Are There Any Specific Directions Regarding the Property or the Sale in the Will?

If the decedent has left specific directions regarding the sale or the disposition of the property, then you should be aware of them.

For example, if the property was specifically bequeathed to an individual, many counties require that, before it is offered for sale, notice has to be given to the person to whom it was bequeathed and court approval obtained. Some counties require seven days notice, some ten, and some even require that the consent of the person be on file. You need to discuss the situation with the attorney for the estate.

Is There Personal Property To Be Included With the Real Property?

If you are aware of personal property to be included in the sale, inform the attorney so that the necessary wording can be included in the published notice. It may also be that the attorney knows of personal property to be included that you or the representative have not considered. Such personal property might include removable appliances such as portable dishwasher, washer, dryer, range, refrigerator, permanent trailers or single wide mobile homes classified as a motor vehicle.

The personal representative may sell personal property and real property as a unit. The personal property and real property need not be appraised as one unit, but can be sold under one bid, if the court finds the sale as a unit to be to the advantage of the estate.

The sale as a unit must not be less than 90 percent of the appraised value (either the sum of the appraised values of both personal and real properties or as a unit). *What constitutes a sale for 90% of the appraised value varies from county to county. Check the local court rules in the appendix.*

The sale must be conducted as in the manner for real property.

What If There Is No Will?

If the decedent did not leave a Will, then a Notice of Sale of Real Property at Private Sale must be published. (See Form 2.) The attorney will handle this procedure. Remember, if you list the property before the notice is published *the property cannot be legally sold until after the date stated in the notice.*

Check Appraisal

Ask the representative or the attorney if the property has been appraised by the probate referee. Why is an appraisal needed in a probate? The appraisal: 1) determines the value for tax purposes so that the gain or loss on sale can be calculated; 2) sets a value in the event the property has to be divided among more than one beneficiary/heir; and 3) establishes a basis to calculate the statutory representative and attorney fees.

Experience has shown me that in most instances the probate referee's appraisal was a solid opinion of the fair market value. However, you should make your own evaluation. If you disagree with the referee's appraisal, discuss the matter with the representative and the attorney. It may be that the attorney will want to approach the referee for a clarification of the valuation, which may then result in a reevaluation.

You should be aware of the court appraised value (probate referee's appraisal) so that you do not present a bid that is less than 90% of the appraised value as set by the probate referee. The court will not confirm a sale of real property unless the bid amount is at least 90% of the appraised value. (Probate Code Section 10309.)

For example:

Appraised value	$200,000
	x 90%
Minimum bid	$180,000

Some counties have a different formula for figuring the minimum bid, taking into account the expenses of sale. Check the local court rules in the appendix and also ask the estate attorney to be sure the bid you are presenting is at or above the minimum amount. Your time and effort will be wasted if you present an offer only to be told that it is too low, not to mention the disappointment of the proposed buyer who submitted the offer.

If, after a diligent sales effort, the property cannot be sold for 90% of the court appraised value, discuss the matter with the representative and the attorney. It is possible to have the property reappraised.

The appraisal by the probate referee *must be within one year* of the date of the sale. The property is appraised as of the date of death, or the date of the appointment of the conservator or guardian. So if it has been a year or close to a year from the date of death or the date of the conservator's or guardian's appointment, discuss the fact with the representative and the attorney. In addition, as you well know, the market can change in a year, and the court may order a reappraisal to make sure the property is being sold at or above fair market value.

The hearing on the confirmation of the sale will be continued if the appraisal is not current. This is an item to which you should pay close attention.

Notice of Sale of Real Property at Private Sale

If there is no Will or if there is a Will which does not contain a power of sale clause, before the property can be legally sold and a bid accepted, if the value of the property is over $5,000, the attorney must cause to be published a Notice of Sale of Real Property at Private Sale. (See Form 2.)

If the value of the real property to be sold is $5,000 or less, the representative can post notice of sale at the courthouse rather than publishing the notice, which saves considerable time. The attorney should handle this procedure.

Publishing the Notice of Sale of Real Property at Private Sale takes approximately three weeks. The listing of the property is premature until this notice is published. The sale cannot take place until on or after the first day stated in the published notice. If time is of the essence, the court may sign an order shortening time for publication to seven days with sale on the eighth day, the practical effect being that only one publication is required. If you have a specific time problem, ask the attorney for the estate if it would be possible to obtain an Order Shortening Publication Time. The court will require extraordinary circumstances to grant the petition.

You can aid the attorney by making sure that he has an accurate legal description and assessor's parcel number for the property to be sold.

Review the notice as published, because it will state the terms of sale. The published notice of sale constitutes a solicitation for offers.

The offer of sale you present to the personal representative must be on the same terms as the published notice. There cannot be a variance in the terms of sale between the notice and the report of sale and bid presented to the court.

If the notice solicits cash offers only, the court cannot confirm a sale on terms other than cash. More latitude in the sale terms is possible if the notice calls for *"cash or such credit terms and conditions as the court may approve."*

If a Report of Sale and Petition for Order Confirming Sale is filed prior to the date of sale specified in the notice, the court cannot announce the sale on the date set for hearing. The court must then deny confirmation without prejudice. The term "without prejudice" leaves the confirmation process open to be corrected and a new petition filed. The offer or acceptance documents must be rewritten and re-signed and a new report of sale filed. The report of sale document is signed by the petitioner under penalty of perjury and therefore the paperwork must be correct.

In addition to creating additional, unnecessary work, the rewriting and re-signing process gives the buyer or seller an opportunity to back out. If the deal falls through at this point you will have put in a lot of hard work for which you will not be paid.

In my experience, this technicality is one of the most common reasons for delay in a probate sale. By reading this book and finetuning your knowledge, you can ensure that your probate sale will proceed efficiently, with less frustration and hassle.

The sale must be made within one year after publication of the notice of sale.

Exclusive Right-to-Sell Listing Agreement

If the representative desires to enter into an exclusive right-to-sell listing agreement, the following must be considered:

If the Representative Has Full Powers Under the IAEA.

If he or she does, an exclusive right-to-sell listing agreement may be granted for a period of not to exceed 90 days *without* giving written Notice of Proposed Action, with one exception: if the original exclusive right to sell and all extensions are more than 270 days, the personal representative must give a written Notice of Proposed Action. The listing broker is not assured a commission unless the listing is exclusive.

If the Representative Does Not Have Full Powers Under the IAEA.

If he or she does not, then an Order Authorizing Execution of Exclusive Right-to-

Sell Listing Agreement must be obtained from the court. (See Form 3 at the end of this chapter.) The order can be obtained "ex-parte," which means that a request to the court does not require a hearing or any notice and can usually be obtained within a day or two of presentation to the court. Request that the attorney obtain a court order authorizing an exclusive right-to-sell listing. Give the attorney for the representative a copy of the proposed listing agreement to attach to the application for the exclusive right-to-sell listing.

The court will authorize an exclusive right to sell the property for a period not in excess of 90 days, upon a showing of necessity and advantage to the estate. (See Chapter 4 for a list of possible reasons why it is advantageous to the estate.) Extensions of the 90-day period will be granted upon an ex-parte application to the court of a showing of necessity and advantage to the estate. Each extension may be for a period not in excess of 90 days.

Some courts do not favor an exclusive right-to-sell agreement. I think the reason for this is that exposure to the market can be generated by persons and circumstances other than by the listing broker in his or her sales efforts. Since a listing broker with an exclusive right-to-sell is guaranteed a commission no matter who produces the buyer, a commission could be paid to a broker who did not find the buyer.

In an intestate estate where the estate representative is required to publish a Notice of

Sale of Real Property at Private Sale in the newspaper, potential buyers and investors read the advertisements and come forth on their own. In that event, with an exclusive right-to-sell, the broker would receive a commission even though he/she did not do the work.

Secondly, the property is automatically exposed when neighbors, friends and acquaintances learn of the property owner's death. A house in need of repairs and paint, as many probate sale houses are, may be a bargain and will attract attention.

On the other hand, where there is a Will with a power of sale, no notice of intention to sell will be published and therefore no exposure. The likelihood of outside purchasers is less and it is simpler for the representative to list the real property for sale through a broker.

Check the appendix to see if the county in which the probate proceeding is located has any local court rules concerning the exclusive right-to-sell listing.

Why Request An Exclusive Listing Agreement?

An exclusive listing broker is assured a commission. In probate sales some courts inquire into the services actually performed by the exclusive listing broker. The exclusive listing performs a valuable service to the estate by listing the property through the multiple listing service which will assure maximum exposure of the property to the market. The California Law Review Commission recommends that the ex-

clusive listing broker be entitled to share in the commission without producing a buyer or showing that he or she has personally made an effort to sell the property. If the listing agreement is not exclusive, some courts may not approve a commission merely for listing the property.

If the representative has authority to administer the estate under the IAEA, then it may not be necessary to obtain court authority or give notice for the exclusive listing; however, the new laws indicate that *in order to be assured of a commission to the listing broker, an exclusive listing is necessary.*

Notice of Proposed Action re Intent to List Property

If the personal representative *does not have full powers* under the IAEA, before the representative signs the listing agreement, a Notice of Proposed Action re intent to list property must be prepared by the attorney and mailed to the interested persons. The notice states that on or after 15 days the representative will list the property with a broker. If the listing agreement is to be exclusive, then the notice should so state. The interested persons then have 15 days to object. If no objections are received, then the listing can proceed. (See Form 4.)

Disclosure Statement Is Not Required

You should be aware that, according to Civil Code Section 1102.1, the requirements for the Real Estate Transfer Disclosure Statement do not apply when:

- The transfer (sale) is ordered by the probate court.
- The transfer is made by a fiduciary (executor, administrator, conservator, guardian or trustee) in the course of the administration of an estate.

In Summary:

If

____ The Will contains a power of sale clause,
or,
if the Will does not contain a power of sale
clause and the Notice of Sale of Real
Property at Private Sale has been published;
and

____ You have checked to see if any personal
property is to be included in the sale;
and

____ You have checked the probate referee's
appraisal;
and

____ You have called the attorney for the
personal representative to make sure
The Notice of Proposed Action re intent to
list property has been mailed to all
interested persons, if necessary;
and

____ The Order for Exclusive Listing Agreement
has been obtained, if the representative
does not have *full* IAEA powers or you want
to be assured the commission;.

then:

You are ready to request the representative to sign the
Listing Agreement and proceed with the sale.

An Orderly Probate Sale

It was determined that the house should be sold so that cash could be distributed to the three daughters of the decedent. The daughters all lived in different areas of the country and it would have been impossible for them to own the house jointly as a rental because they were not in agreement on many subjects.

Since the executor was a business acquaintance of the decedent and her handling of the estate would be under scrutiny of the three daughters, her attorney advised her it was important that she handle all procedures strictly according to the law and with court approval, in order to avoid any personal liability.

The Will contained a power of sale clause, so it was not necessary to publish a Notice of Sale of Real Property at Private Sale.

The executor then contacted a real estate agent. Together they discussed the selling price and the court appraised value. Before she signed the listing agreement she contacted her attorney. The selling agent also contacted the attorney.

The attorney told the executor that a notice had to be sent to the daughters before she could list the property and that an order for an exclusive listing agreement must be obtained from the court.

The attorney then prepared the Notice of Proposed Action re intent to list property and mailed it to the daughters, giving the daughters the statutory period of time (15 days) in which they could object to the sale, the selling price or the listing broker. During the same interval of time, the attorney petitioned and received from the court the order for an exclusive listing agreement.

After the 15-day notice period expired, the executor signed the listing agreement and the sales agent proceeded with the sale. During the 15-day period the real estate agent, having knowledge of the pending listing, verified the ownership through a title company, researched comparable sales and listings and generally surveyed the area. During an open house held the first weekend after the listing agreement was signed, the house sold for more than the court appraised value.

The Report of Sale and Petition for Order Confirming Sale of Real Property was filed by the attorney. There were no overbids at the hearing and the sale was approved by the court.

Everyone concerned was pleased with the manner in which this sale was expeditiously handled.

Notice of Sale of Real Property at Private Sale
No. 10000

In the Superior Court of the State of California, for the County of Comfort.

In the Matter of the Estate of N. O. Longerhere, Deceased.

Notice is hereby given that the undersigned will sell at Private Sale, to the highest and best bidder, subject to confirmation of said Superior Court, on or after the 10th day of September, 1989 at the office of JOHN Q. LAWYER, 100 City Justice Building, Suite 200, Heavenly, California 90000, County of Comfort, State of California, all the right, title and interest of said deceased at the time of death and all the right, title and interest that the estate of said deceased has acquired by operation of law or otherwise, other than or in addition to that of said deceased, at the time of death, in and to all the certain real property, situated in the City of Heavenly, County of Comfort, State of California, particularly described as follows, to-wit:

Lot 101 in Block 5, as designed on the map entitled "Heavenly Ranchos, Heavenly, California", which map was filed in the office of the Recorder of the County of Comfort, State of California, on February 29, 1942, in Volume 26 of maps, at plate 916

More Commonly known as: 10 Best Place, Heavenly, California 90000.

Terms of sale cash in lawful money of the United States on confirmation of sale, on any terms acceptable to the executor. Ten percent of amount bid to be deposited with bid.

Bids or offers to be in writing and will be received at the aforesaid office at any time after the first publication hereof and before date of sale.

Dated this 20th day of August, 1989

I.M. STANDIN, Executor of the Will of said Decedent.

JOHN Q. LAWYER
100 City Justice Bldg., Ste. 200
Heavenly, CA 90000

Sample provided by the Daily Journal Corp., California's largest publisher of legal newspapers.

Form 2
Notice of Sale of Real Property at Private Sale

JOHN Q. LAWYER
Attorney at Law
100 City Justice Building
Suite 200
Heavenly, California 90000

415-100-1000

Attorney for Petitioner

SUPERIOR COURT OF CALIFORNIA, COUNTY OF COMFORT

ESTATE OF	)	NO. 10000
	)	
N. O. LONGERHERE,	)	ORDER AUTHORIZING
	)	EXECUTION
	)	OF EXCLUSIVE RIGHT-TO-SELL
	)	LISTING AGREEMENT
Deceased.	)	
	)	

    The verified petition of I. M. STANDIN, the Personal Representative of the within Estate, having been previously presented and heard and proof being made to the satisfaction of the Court, the Court finds that notice of the hearing should be dispensed with; that it is for the advantage, benefit and best interest of the within Estate and those interested herein that I. M. STANDIN be authorized to grant an exclusive right to sell the real property as hereinafter described.

    IT IS THEREFORE ORDERED, ADJUDGED AND DECREED that notice of the hearing on said petition be, and is hereby, dispensed with.

Form 3, Page 1
Order Authorizing Execution of Exclusive Listing Agreement

IT IS ORDERED THAT said I. M. STANDIN be, and is hereby authorized to execute and deliver that certain written contract exemplified by Exhibit A attached to the petition, whereby the Personal Representative grants DECADE 40 REAL ESTATE, a licensed real estate brokerage, an exclusive right-to-sell listing to sell the property therein described upon the terms and conditions therein set forth.

IT IS FURTHER ORDERED, ADJUDGED AND DECREED that said exclusive listing shall provide for the payment of a real estate broker's commission of such amount as may be allowed by the Court upon confirmation of a sale, not to exceed 6% of the total sales price.

Dated: September 10, 1989.

_____
JUDGE OF THE SUPERIOR COURT

(For Exhibit A, the Listing Agreement, see Form 5)

Form 3, Page 2
Order Authorizing Execution of Exclusive Listing Agreement

ATTORNEY OR PARTY WITHOUT ATTORNEY (Name and Address):	TELEPHONE NO.: (415) 100-1000	FOR COURT USE ONLY
JOHN Q. LAWYER 100 City Justice Building Suite 200 Heavenly, CA 90000 ATTORNEY FOR (Name): Petitioner		

SUPERIOR COURT OF CALIFORNIA, COUNTY OF COMFORT
STREET ADDRESS: Court Building
MAILING ADDRESS: Court Building
CITY AND ZIP CODE: Heavenly, CA 900000
BRANCH NAME:

ESTATE OF (NAME): N. O. LONGERHERE

DECEDENT

NOTICE OF PROPOSED ACTION Independent Administration of Estates Act Objection – Consent	CASE NUMBER: 10000

NOTICE: If you do not object in writing or obtain a court order preventing the action proposed below, you will be treated as if you consented to the proposed action and you may not object after the proposed action has been taken. If you object, the personal representative may take the proposed action only under court supervision. An objection form is on the reverse. If you wish to object, you may use the form or prepare your own written objection.

1. The personal representative (executor or administrator) of the estate of the deceased is (names):
   I. M. STANDIN

2. The personal representative has authority to administer the estate without court supervision under the Independent Administration of Estates Act (Probate Code section 10400 et seq.)
   a. ☐ with full authority under the act.
   b. ☒ with limited authority under the act (there is no authority, without court supervision, to (1) sell or exchange real property or (2) grant an option to purchase real property or (3) borrow money with the loan secured by an encumbrance upon real property)

3. On or after (date): [   ], the personal representative will take the following action without court supervision (describe in specific terms here or in Attachment 3):
   ☐ The proposed action is described in an attachment labeled Attachment 3.

   Petition the court for an order authorizing an exclusive listing to list the real property located at 10 Best Place, Heavenly, California 90000 with DECADE 40 Real Estate, said listing to be exclusive. A copy of the proposed listing agreement is attached hereto, marked Exhibit A and made a part hereof. Listing price of property to be $200,000. Six percent (6%) sales commission.

4. ☒ Real property transaction (Check this box and complete item 4b if the proposed action involves a sale or exchange or a grant of an option to purchase real property.)
   a. The material terms of the transaction are specified in item 3, including any sale price and the amount of or method of calculating any commission or compensation to an agent or broker.
   b. $ 200,000   is the value of the subject property in the probate inventory. ☐ No inventory yet.

NOTICE: A sale of real property without court supervision means that the sale will NOT be presented to the court for confirmation at a hearing at which higher bids for the property may be presented and the property sold to the highest bidder.

(Continued on reverse)

Form Approved by the
Judicial Council of California
DE-165 (Rev. July 1, 1988)

NOTICE OF PROPOSED ACTION
Objection – Consent
(Probate)

Probate Code, § 10580 et seq.

Form 4, Page 1

ESTATE OF (NAME): N. O. LONGERHERE		CASE NUMBER:
	DECEDENT	10000

5. If you OBJECT to the proposed action

   a. Sign the objection form below and deliver or mail it to the personal representative at the following address (*specify name and address*): John Q. Lawyer
                    100 City Justice Building, Suite 200
                    Heavenly, CA 90000

     – OR –

   b. Send your own written objection to the address in item 5a. (*Be sure to identify the proposed action and state that you object to it.*)

     – OR –

   c. Apply to the court for an order preventing the personal representative from taking the proposed action without court supervision.

   d. NOTE: Your written objection or the court order must be received by the personal representative before the date in the box in item 3, or before the proposed action is taken, whichever is later. If you object, the personal representative may take the proposed action only under court supervision.

6. If you APPROVE the proposed action, you may sign the consent form below and return it to the address in item 5a. If you do not object in writing or obtain a court order, you will be treated as if you consented to the proposed action.

7. If you need more INFORMATION, call (*name*): John Q. Lawyer
                       (*telephone*): (415) 100-1000

Date:

JOHN Q. LAWYER

         (TYPE OR PRINT NAME)   ▶   (SIGNATURE OF PERSONAL REPRESENTATIVE OR ATTORNEY)

OBJECTION TO PROPOSED ACTION

☐ I OBJECT to the action proposed above in item 3.

NOTICE: Sign and return this form (both sides) to the address in item 5a. The form must be received before the date in the box in item 3, or before the proposed action is taken, whichever is later. (*You may want to use certified mail, with return receipt requested. Make a copy of this form for your records.*)

Date:

         (TYPE OR PRINT NAME)   ▶   (SIGNATURE OF OBJECTOR)

CONSENT TO PROPOSED ACTION

☐ I CONSENT to the action proposed above in item 3.

NOTICE: You may indicate your **consent** by signing and returning this form (both sides) to the address in item 5a. If you do not object in writing or obtain a court order, you will be treated as if you consented to the proposed action.

Date:

         (TYPE OR PRINT NAME)   ▶   (SIGNATURE OF CONSENTER)

DE-165 (Rev. July 1, 1988)   NOTICE OF PROPOSED ACTION   Page two
Objection – Consent
(Probate)

Form 4, Page 2

NOTES

Chapter 4

The Listing Agreement

 Now that the Order for an Exclusive Listing has been obtained, if necessary, and you have done your homework, you are ready for the client to sign the listing agreement. In order to conduct the business of the estate and sell the property, the representative may enter into a written contract with a licensed real estate broker, who may associate other licensed real estate brokers. The multiple listing service may also be used. (Remember that under the Independent Administration of Estates Act, if the personal representative has full IAEA powers, you can sidestep the court's approval. See Chapter 2.)

Since the forms of listing agreements vary from broker to broker, only the provisions applicable to probate sales will be addressed here.

Preparing the Listing Agreement

You should consider the following items:

Exclusive Listing Agreement.

Is the listing agreement to be exclusive? An exclusive listing is recommended to assure your commission. (See Chapter 3.)

Subject to Court Confirmation.

The listing agreement should contain the words: *"Sale subject to court confirmation"*; or, if sold under the Independent Administration of Estates Act, *"Sale subject to consent of all*

*heirs or beneficiaries or subject to court confir-
mation.*" You can insert this term in the "Additional Terms" section of the agreement. (See
Form 5 at the end of this chapter.) It is a good
idea to state that the sale is subject to court
confirmation even if the sale will take place
under the IAEA, in case the representative
decides at a later time to ask for confirmation.

Commission If Sale Is Subject to Court Confirmation.

A request for the approval of your commission will be contained in the Report of Sale
and Petition for Order Confirming Sale of Real
Property. (See Chapter 5.) Under the new law,
the sale must be confirmed or approved by the
court to assure your commission. *Even though
the contract may specify a certain commission,
the court retains the final authority to set the
amount of the commission to be received.*

The amount of commission varies from
county to county according to local court policy,
which takes into account local community
standards. Check the appendix in this book for
the local policy for each county in California.
Also, ask the attorney for the estate what the
current policy is in the county in which your sale
is located, in case there have been recent changes.

Presently, the general policy in most counties is to allow 6% on improved property and
10% on the sale of raw land. However, Los
Angeles County usually will only approve a 5%
commission on the sale of improved property
with the exception of 6% on the sale of a small
improved parcel.

Some aspects of the commission structure changed as of July 1, 1988. Probate Code Section 10161, which deals with court-determined reasonable compensation for the broker, is very clear and concise:

a. Subject to the provisions of this article, whether or not the agent or broker has a contract with the personal representative, the fee, commission, or other compensation of an agent or broker in connection with a sale of property shall be the amount the court, in its discretion, determines to be a reasonable compensation for the services of the agent or broker to the estate.

b. Unless the agent or broker holds a contract granting an exclusive right to sell the property, an agent or broker is not entitled to any fee, commission, or other compensation for services to the estate in connection with a sale except in the following cases:

1. Where the agent or broker produces the original bid which is returned to the court for confirmation.

2. Where the property is sold on an increased bid, made at the time of the hearing on the petition for confirmation, to a purchaser procured by the agent or broker.

3. If the agent or broker has a contract with the personal representative, the amount of the compensation of the agent or broker in connection with the sale of property shall not exceed the amount provided for in the contract.

The amount of commission may not exceed the amount provided in the contract, even though the applicable court rules may allow a higher commission. As part of your homework before negotiating the contract with the representative, call the attorney for the estate and find out the maximum commission the court will approve. Using this knowledge will increase the chances that the sale will be confirmed by the court with no delay, and will ensure that you receive the maximum commission possible.

Keep in mind that a commission may be paid for the sale of personal property, in the event personal property is to be included in the sale.

You should also be aware that the representative is not personally liable on the contract. No liability of any kind, including payment of a commission, is incurred by the estate under the contract or a sale unless (Probate Code Sections 10150[b] and 10160):

- An actual sale is made.
- If court confirmation or approval is required, the sale is confirmed or approved by the court as required.
- The sale is consummated. (*Exception:* personal property where no court confirmation is required. Probate Code Section 10259. See also Probate Code Section 10160.)

Since you don't yet have a buyer, there is no reason at this point for you to be concerned with the division of the commission. Examples of how the commission will be divided in various situations involving another broker or agent representing the buyer or an overbidder are contained in Chapter 5.

Commission If Sale Is NOT Subject to Court Confirmation.

In this instance, when the sale is taking place under the IAEA, the commission is handled as it is during a non-probate listing. The percentage and terms are agreed upon between the listing agent and the personal representative and stated in the listing agreement. The court will not be determining the amount and division of the commission.

Listing Agreement About to Expire

If the listing agreement is due to expire and the property has not been sold, one or two extensions to the exclusive listing may be granted. Each extension cannot exceed 90 days. A showing of necessity and advantage to the estate must be made.

At least three weeks before the listing agreement will expire, obtain the agreement of the representative to extend the listing.

If the representative *has full powers* under the IAEA and the original exclusive right to sell and all extensions total less than 270 days, no written notice must be given and you can proceed with the renewal of the listing agreement. But, if the original exclusive right to sell and all extensions add up to more than 270 days, a written Notice of Proposed Action must be given.

Remember, though, that the listing must be exclusive to assure a commission.

Contact the attorney for the representative to make sure the Notice of Proposed

Examples of necessity and advantage to the estate of an exclusive listing:

- Unlikely the estate would find a broker willing to properly market the property without an exclusive listing agreement.
- Past unsuccessful exposure.
- Condition of property and/or neighborhood.
- Out-of-county residence of personal representative.
- Listing agreement contract which predates the establishment of the court proceeding; that is, the decedent had the property up for sale and died before the property could be sold.

Action has been given before you proceed to renew the listing agreement.

If the personal representative *does not have full powers* under the IAEA, then court approval must be obtained. Contact the attorney for the representative and ask the attorney to prepare the necessary application to the court to have the exclusive listing agreement extended.

EXCLUSIVE AUTHORIZATION AND RIGHT TO SELL
THIS IS INTENDED TO BE A LEGALLY BINDING AGREEMENT — READ IT CAREFULLY.
CALIFORNIA ASSOCIATION OF REALTORS® (CAR) STANDARD FORM

1. **EXCLUSIVE RIGHT TO SELL:** I hereby employ and grant _____ DECADE 40 REAL ESTATE
hereinafter called "Broker," the exclusive and irrevocable right commencing on ____ September 15 ____, 19 89 , and expiring at
midnight on ____ March 14 ____, 19 90 , to sell or exchange the real property situated in the City of ____ Heavenly ____,
County of ____ Comfort ____, California described as follows: ____ Lot 101 in Block 5, ____
Heavenly Valley Ranchos, Heavenly, CA 90000

2. **TERMS OF SALE:** The purchase price shall be ____ Two Hundred Thousand Dollars ____
____ ($ 200,000.00 ____), to be paid as follows ____ cash, cash to new ____
loan

   The following items of personal property are included in the above stated price: ____ none ____ .

3. **TITLE INSURANCE:** Evidence of title shall be a California Land Title Association policy of title insurance in the amount of the selling price.

Notice: The amount or rate of real estate commissions is not fixed by law. They are set by each Broker individually and may be negotiable between the Seller and Broker.

4. **COMPENSATION TO BROKER:** I hereby agree to compensate Broker, irrespective of agency relationship(s), as follows:
   (a) ____ 6 ____ percent of the selling price, or $ ____ --- ____ , if the property is sold during the term hereof, or any extension thereof, by Broker or through any other person, or by me on the terms herein set forth, or any other price and terms I may accept, or ____ -- ____ percent of the price shown in 2, or $ ____ -- ____ , if said property is withdrawn from sale, transferred, conveyed, leased, or rented without the consent of Broker, or made unmarketable by my voluntary act during the term hereof or any extension thereof.
   (b) The compensation provided for in subparagraph (a) above if property is sold, conveyed or otherwise transferred within ____ 45 ____ calendar days after the termination of this authority or any extension thereof to anyone with whom Broker has had negotiations prior to final termination, provided I have received notice in writing, including the names of the prospective purchasers, before or upon termination of this agreement or any extension hereof. However, I shall not be obligated to pay the compensation provided for in subparagraph (a) if a valid listing agreement is entered into during the term of said protection period with another licensed real estate broker and a sale, lease or exchange of the property is made during the term of said valid listing agreement.
   (c) I authorize Broker to cooperate with other brokers, to appoint subagents, and to divide with other brokers such compensation in any manner acceptable to brokers.
   (d) In the event of an exchange, permission is hereby given Broker to represent all parties and collect compensation or commissions from them, provided there is full disclosure to all principals of such agency. Broker is authorized to divide with other brokers such compensation or commissions in any manner acceptable to brokers.
   (e) Seller shall execute and deliver an escrow instruction irrevocably assigning Broker's compensation in an amount equal to the compensation provided in subparagraph (a) (above) from the Seller's proceeds.

5. **DEPOSIT:** Broker is authorized to accept and hold on Seller's behalf a deposit to be applied toward purchase price.

6. **HOME PROTECTION PLAN:** Seller is informed that home protection plans are available. Such plans may provide additional protection and benefit to a Seller and Buyer. Cost and coverage may vary.

*7. **KEYBOX:** I authorize Broker to install a KEYBOX:
   Refer to reverse side for important keybox information.   (Initial) YES (IMS) NO (/)

8. **SIGN:** Authorization to install a FOR SALE/SOLD sign on the property: (Initial) YES (IMS) NO (/)

9. **PEST CONTROL:** Seller shall furnish a current Structural Pest Control Report of the main building
   and all structures of the property, except ____ -- ____   (Initial) YES (IMS) NO (/)

10. **DISCLOSURE:** Unless exempt, Seller shall provide a Real Estate Transfer Disclosure Statement concerning the condition of the property. I agree to save and hold Broker harmless from all claims, disputes, litigation, and/or judgments arising from any incorrect information supplied by me, or from any material fact known by me which I fail to disclose.

*11. **TAX WITHHOLDING:** Seller agrees to perform any act reasonably necessary to carry out the provisions of FIRPTA (Internal Revenue Code §1445) and California   (Initial) (IMS)
   Revenue and Taxation Code §§18805 and 26131, and regulations promulgated thereunder. Refer to the reverse side for withholding provisions and exemptions.

12. **EQUAL HOUSING OPPORTUNITY:** This property is offered in compliance with federal, state, and local anti-discrimination laws.

Form 5-A, Page 1
Listing Agreement: IAEA

* 13. **ARBITRATION OF DISPUTES:** Any dispute or claim in law or equity arising out of this contract or any resulting transaction shall be decided by neutral binding arbitration in accordance with the rules of the American Arbitration Association, and not by court action except as provided by California law for judicial review of arbitration proceedings. Judgment upon the award rendered by the arbitrator(s) may be entered in any court having jurisdiction thereof. The parties shall have the right to discovery in accordance with Code of Civil Procedure §1283.05. The following matters are excluded from arbitration hereunder: (a) a judicial or non-judicial foreclosure or other action or proceeding to enforce a deed of trust, mortgage, or real property sales contract as defined in Civil Code §2985, (b) an unlawful detainer action, (c) the filing or enforcement of a mechanic's lien, (d) any matter which is within the jurisdiction of a probate court, or (e) an action for bodily injury or wrongful death, or for latent or patent defects to which Code of Civil Procedure §337.1 or §337.15 applies. The filing of a judicial action to enable the recording of a notice of pending action, for order of attachment, receivership, injunction, or other provisional remedies, shall not constitute a waiver of the right to arbitrate under this provision.

"NOTICE: BY INITIALLING IN THE SPACE BELOW YOU ARE AGREEING TO HAVE ANY DISPUTE ARISING OUT OF THE MATTERS INCLUDED IN THE 'ARBITRATION OF DISPUTES' PROVISION DECIDED BY NEUTRAL ARBITRATION AS PROVIDED BY CALIFORNIA LAW AND YOU ARE GIVING UP ANY RIGHTS YOU MIGHT POSSESS TO HAVE THE DISPUTE LITIGATED IN A COURT OR JURY TRIAL. BY INITIALLING IN THE SPACE BELOW YOU ARE GIVING UP YOUR JUDICIAL RIGHTS TO DISCOVERY AND APPEAL, UNLESS THOSE RIGHTS ARE SPECIFICALLY INCLUDED IN THE 'ARBITRATION OF DISPUTES' PROVISION. IF YOU REFUSE TO SUBMIT TO ARBITRATION AFTER AGREEING TO THIS PROVISION, YOU MAY BE COMPELLED TO ARBITRATE UNDER THE AUTHORITY OF THE CALIFORNIA CODE OF CIVIL PROCEDURE. YOUR AGREEMENT TO THIS ARBITRATION PROVISION IS VOLUNTARY."

"WE HAVE READ AND UNDERSTAND THE FOREGOING AND AGREE TO SUBMIT DISPUTES ARISING OUT OF THE MATTERS INCLUDED IN THE 'ARBITRATION OF DISPUTES' PROVISION TO NEUTRAL ARBITRATION."

(Initial) BROKER (D4RE) SELLER (IMS /)

14. **ATTORNEY'S FEES:** In any action, proceeding or arbitration arising out of this agreement, the prevailing party shall be entitled to reasonable attorney's fees and costs.

15. **ADDITIONAL TERMS:** Sale subject to consent of all heirs/beneficiaries or confirmation of court.

16. **ENTIRE AGREEMENT:** I, the Seller, warrant that I am the owner of the property or have the authority to execute this agreement. The Seller and Broker further intend that this agreement constitutes the complete and exclusive statement of its terms and that no extrinsic evidence whatsoever may be introduced in any judicial or arbitration proceeding, if any, involving this agreement.

I acknowledge that I have read and understand this agreement, including the information on the reverse side, and have received a copy.

17. **CAPTIONS:** The Captions in this agreement are for convenience of reference only and are not intended as part of this agreement.

Date September 15 , 19 89 Heavenly , California
Seller I.M. STANDIN, Exec/Will of N.O. LONGERHERE Address 20 Responsible Lane
Seller City Heavenly State CA Phone 123-4567

In consideration of the above, Broker agrees to use diligence in procuring a purchaser.
Real Estate Broker Decade 40 Real Estate By W. E. Sell
Address #1 Profitable Row City Heavenly, CA Date 9/15/89

THIS STANDARDIZED DOCUMENT FOR USE IN SIMPLE TRANSACTIONS HAS BEEN APPROVED BY THE CALIFORNIA ASSOCIATION OF REALTORS* IN FORM ONLY. NO REPRESENTATION IS MADE AS TO THE APPROVAL OF THE FORM OF ANY SUPPLEMENTS NOT CURRENTLY PUBLISHED BY THE CALIFORNIA ASSOCIATION OF REALTORS* OR THE LEGAL VALIDITY OR ADEQUACY OF ANY PROVISION IN ANY SPECIFIC TRANSACTION. IT SHOULD NOT BE USED IN COMPLEX TRANSACTIONS OR WITH EXTENSIVE RIDERS OR ADDITIONS.

A REAL ESTATE BROKER IS THE PERSON QUALIFIED TO ADVISE ON REAL ESTATE TRANSACTIONS. IF YOU DESIRE LEGAL OR TAX ADVICE, CONSULT AN APPROPRIATE PROFESSIONAL.

This form is available for use by the entire real estate industry. The use of this form is not intended to identify the user as a REALTOR*. REALTOR* is a registered collective membership mark which may be used only by real estate licensees who are members of the NATIONAL ASSOCIATION OF REALTORS* and who subscribe to its Code of Ethics.

┌─────────────── OFFICE USE ONLY ───────────────┐
Reviewed by Broker or Designee _____
Date ___ __ ____

* REFER TO REVERSE SIDE FOR ADDITIONAL INFORMATION
Copyright 1988, CALIFORNIA ASSOCIATION OF REALTORS*
525 South Virgil Avenue, Los Angeles, California 90020
Revised 3/89

FORM AL-14

Form 5-A, Page 2
Listing Agreement: IAEA

7. **KEYBOX:** A keybox designed as a repository of a key to the above premises, will permit access to the interior of the premises by Participants of the Multiple Listing Service (MLS), their authorized licensees and prospective buyers. If property is not seller occupied, seller shall be responsible for obtaining occupants' written permission for use of the keybox. Neither listing nor selling broker, MLS or Board of REALTORS® is an insurer against theft, loss, vandalism or damage attributed to the use of keybox. SELLER is advised to verify the existence of, or obtain appropriate insurance through their own insurance broker.

11. **TAX WITHHOLDING:** Under the Foreign Investment in Real Property Tax Act (FIRPTA), IRC 1445, *every* Buyer of U.S. real property *must*, unless an exemption applies, deduct and withhold from Seller's proceeds 10% of the gross sales price. Under California Revenue and Taxation Code §§18805 and 26131, the Buyer must deduct and withhold an additional one-third of the amount required to be withheld under federal law. The primary FIRPTA exemptions are: No withholding is required if (a) Seller provides Buyer with an affidavit under penalty of perjury, that Seller is not a "foreign person," or (b) Seller provides Buyer with a "qualifying statement" issued by the Internal Revenue Service, or (c) Buyer purchases real property for use as a residence and the purchase price is $300,000 or less and if Buyer or a member of Buyer's family has definite plans to reside at the property for at least 50% of the number of days it is in use during each of the first two twelve-month periods after transfer. Seller agrees to execute and deliver as directed any instrument, affidavit or statement, reasonably necessary to carry out those statutes and regulations promulgated thereunder.

13. **ARBITRATION:** Arbitration is the referral of a dispute to one or more impartial persons for final and binding determination. It is private and informal, designed for quick, practical, and inexpensive settlements. Arbitration is an orderly proceeding, governed by rules of procedure and standards of conduct prescribed by law.

ENFORCEMENT OF ARBITRATION AGREEMENTS
UNDER CALIFORNIA CODE OF CIVIL PROCEDURE SECTIONS 1281, 1282.4, 1283.1, 1283.05, 1287.4 & 1287.6

§ 1281. A written agreement to submit to arbitration an existing controversy or a controversy thereafter arising is valid, enforceable and irreversible, save upon such grounds as exist for the revocation of any contract.

§ 1282.4. A party to the arbitration has the right to be represented by an attorney at any proceeding or hearing in arbitration under this title. A waiver of this right may be revoked; but if a party revokes such waiver, the other party is entitled to a reasonable continuance for the purpose of procuring an attorney.

§ 1283.1. (a) All of the provisions of Section 1283.05 shall be conclusively deemed to be incorporated into, made a part of, and shall be applicable to, every agreement to arbitrate any dispute, controversy, or issue arising out of or resulting from any injury to, or death of, a person caused by the wrongful act or neglect of another.
   (b) Only if the parties by their agreement so provide, may the provisions of Section 1283.05 be incorporated into, made a part of, or made applicable to, any other arbitration agreement.

§ 1283.05. To the extent provided in Section 1283.1 depositions may be taken and discovery obtained in arbitration proceedings as follows:
   (a) After the appointment of the arbitrator or arbitrators, the parties to the arbitration shall have the right to take depositions and to obtain discovery regarding the subject matter of the arbitration, and, to that end, to use and exercise all of the same rights, remedies, and procedures, and be subject to all of the same duties, liabilities, and obligations in the arbitration with respect to the subject matter thereof, as provided in Chapter 2 (commencing with Section 1985) of, and Article 3 (commencing with Section 2016) of Chapter 3 of, Title 3 of Part 4 of this code, as if the subject matter of the arbitration were pending in a civil action before a superior court of this state, subject to the limitations as to depositions set forth in subdivision (e) of this section.
   (b) The arbitrator or arbitrators themselves shall have power, in addition to the power of determining the merits of the arbitration, to enforce the rights, remedies, procedures, duties, liabilities, and obligations of discovery by the imposition of the same terms, conditions, consequences, liabilities, sanctions, and penalties as can be or may be imposed in like circumstances in a civil action by a superior court of this state under the provisions of this code, except the power to order the arrest or imprisonment of a person.
   (c) The arbitrator or arbitrators may consider, determine, and make such orders imposing such terms, conditions, consequences, liabilities, sanctions, and penalties, whenever necessary or appropriate at any time or stage in the course of the arbitration, and such orders shall be as conclusive, final, and enforceable as an arbitration award on the merits, if the making of any such order that is equivalent to an award or correction of an award is subject to the same conditions, if any, as are applicable to the making of an award or correction of an award.
   (d) For the purpose of enforcing the duty to make discovery, to produce evidence or information, including books and records, and to produce persons to testify at a deposition or at a hearing, and to impose terms, conditions, consequences, liabilities, sanctions, and penalties upon a party for violation of any such duty, such party shall be deemed to include every affiliate of such party as defined in this section. For such purpose:
   (1) The personnel of every such affiliate shall be deemed to be the officers, directors, managing agents, agents, and employees of such party to the same degree as each of them, respectively, bears such status to such affiliate; and
   (2) The files, books, and records of every such affiliate shall be deemed to be in the possession and control of, and capable of production by, such party. As used in this section, "affiliate" of the party to the arbitration means and includes any party or person for whose immediate benefit the action or proceeding is prosecuted or defended, or an officer, director, superintendent, member, agent, employee, or managing agent of such party or persons.
   (e) Depositions for discovery shall not be taken unless leave to do so is first granted by the arbitrator or arbitrators.

§ 1287.4. If an award is confirmed, judgment shall be entered in conformity therewith. The judgment so entered has the same force and effect as, and is subject to all the provisions of law relating to, a judgment in a civil action; and it may be enforced like any other judgment of the court in which it is entered.

§ 1287.6. An award that has not been confirmed or vacated has the same force and effect as a contract in writing between the parties to the arbitration.

Form 5-A, Page 3
Listing Agreement: IAEA

EXCLUSIVE AUTHORIZATION AND RIGHT TO SELL
(Sale Requiring Probate Court Confirmation.)
CALIFORNIA ASSOCIATION OF REALTORS® (CAR) STANDARD FORM

1. **EXCLUSIVE RIGHT TO SELL:** The undersigned, hereinafter called "Seller," the duly appointed executor(s) or administrator(s) of the estate of _____N. O. LONGERHERE_____ , Deceased, hereby employs and grants _____DECADE 40 REAL ESTATE_____ , hereinafter called "Broker," the exclusive and irrevocable right commencing on _September 15_ , 19_89_ and expiring at midnight on _March 14_ , 19_90_ (not to exceed 90 days), to sell the real property situated in the City of _____Heavenly_____ , County of_____Comfort_____ , California, described as follows: _10 Best Place, legally described as Lot 101 in Block 5, of Heavenly Ranchos, California, which map was filed in the office of the county recorder on 2/29/42 in volume 6 of maps, at page 916._

2. **TERMS OF SALE:** The purchase price shall be _____Two Hundred Thousand Dollars_____ Dollars ($_200,000.00_), to be paid as follows: _cash, cash to new loan,_

   The following items of personal property are included in the above stated price:_____

   Notice: The amount or rate of real estate commissions is not fixed by law. They are set by each broker individually and may be negotiable between the Seller and Broker.

3. **COMPENSATION TO BROKER:** I hereby agree to compensate Broker as follows:
   (a) From the proceeds of the sale, __6__ percent of the selling price, or $ _____ , or an amount determined by the Court.
   (b) Broker is authorized to cooperate with other brokers, and to divide compensation with other brokers in any manner acceptable to brokers, or as allowed/determined by the Court.
   (c) Compensation is payable irrespective of agency relationship(s) in any resulting transaction, subject to the provisions of the California Probate Code.

4. **DEPOSIT:** Broker is hereby authorized to accept a deposit of _10%_ percent of the purchase price.

5. **AUTHORIZATION OF AGREEMENT:** The undersigned Seller ☐ has Court authority to enter into this agreement, or ☒ on or before _November 15_ 19_89_ Seller will request the Court to authorize this agreement.

6. **CONFIRMATION OF SALE:** Court confirmation of sale is required. No liability of any kind shall be incurred by the estate or Seller under this contract unless a sale is confirmed by the Court.

7. **MULTIPLE LISTING SERVICE (MLS):** Broker is a Participant of_____Heavenly_____ ASSOCIATION/BOARD OF REALTORS® Multiple Listing Service (MLS). Upon Court authorization of this agreement, this listing information will be provided to the MLS to be published and disseminated to its Participants in accordance with its Rules and Regulations. Broker is authorized to cooperate with other real estate brokers, to appoint subagents and to report the sale, its price, terms and financing for the publication, dissemination, information and use by authorized Association/Board members, MLS Participants, and Subscribers.

Form 5-B, Page 1
Listing Agreement: Court Confirmation Required

8. **KEYBOX:** Seller authorizes Broker to install a KEYBOX.   (Initial) YES (_IMS_/____)   NO (____/____)
REFER TO REVERSE SIDE FOR IMPORTANT INFORMATION.
9. **SIGN:** Seller authorizes Broker to place a FOR SALE/SOLD sign on the property. (Initial) YES (_IMS_/____)   NO (____/____)
10. **TAX WITHHOLDING:** Seller agrees to perform any act reasonably necessary to carry out the provisions of FIRPTA (Internal Revenue Code § 1445) and California Revenue and Taxation Code § § 18805 and 26131, and regulations promulgated thereunder. REFER TO REVERSE SIDE FOR IMPORTANT INFORMATION.
11. **EQUAL HOUSING OPPORTUNITY:** This property is offered in compliance with federal, state, and local anti-discrimination laws.
12. **ATTORNEY'S FEES:** In any action, proceeding, or arbitration arising out of this agreement the prevailing party shall be entitled to reasonable attorney's fees and costs.
13. **DISCLOSURE:** Seller and Broker shall disclose to prospective buyers all known material facts affecting the desirability and value of the property. Seller is exempt from providing a Real Estate Transfer Disclosure Statement under California Civil Code § 1102, et seq.
14. **ADDITIONAL TERMS:** _None_

I acknowledge that I have read and understand this agreement, including the information on the reverse side, and have received a copy.

Date: _September 15_____ , 19_90_   _____ _Heavenly_ _____ , California

Seller _ I. M. STANDIN _____   Address _20 Responsible Lane_____

Executor / Administrator of the Estate of   City _Heavenly_ State _CA_ Phone _123-4567_

N. O. LONGERHERE _____ , Deceased

In consideration of the above, Broker agrees to use diligence in procuring a purchaser.

Real Estate Broker _ DECADE 40 REAL ESTATE _ By _ W. E. SELL _____

Address _ #1 Profitable Row _ City _Heavenly, CA 90000_ Date _9/15/89_

FORM AP-14

┌─ OFFICE USE ONLY ─┐
Reviewed by Broker or Designee _____
Date _____

SF-Mar-89

Form 5-B, Page 2
Listing Agreement: Court Confirmation Required

8. **KEYBOX:** A keybox designed as a repository of a key to the above premises, will permit access to the interior of the premises by Participants of the Multiple Listing Service (MLS), their authorized licensees and prospective buyers. If property is not seller occupied, seller shall be responsible for obtaining occupants' written permission for use of the keybox. Neither listing nor selling broker, MLS or Board of REALTORS® is an insurer against theft, loss, vandalism or damage attributed to the use of keybox. SELLER is advised to verify the existence of, or obtain appropriate insurance through their own insurance broker.

10. **TAX WITHHOLDING:** Under the Foreign Investment in Real Property Tax Act (FIRPTA), IRC 1445, *every* Buyer of U.S. real property *must,* unless an exemption applies, deduct and withhold from Seller's proceeds 10% of the gross sales price. Under California Revenue and Taxation Code §§ 18805 and 26131, the Buyer must deduct and withhold an additional one-third of the amount required to be withheld under federal law. The primary FIRPTA exemptions are: No withholding is required if (a) Seller provides Buyer with an affidavit under penalty of perjury, that Seller is not a "foreign person," or (b) provides Buyer with a "qualifying statement" issued by the Internal Revenue Service, or (c) Buyer purchases real property for use as a residence and the purchase price is $300,000 or less and if Buyer or a member of Buyer's family has definite plans to reside at the property for at least 50% of the number of days it is in use during each of the first two twelve-month periods after transfer. Seller agrees to execute and deliver as directed any instrument, affidavit or statement, reasonably necessary to carry out the provisions of FIRPTA and Cal. R. & T. Code and regulations promulgated thereunder.

NOTES

"Expose the property to the market."

Chapter 5

Accepting an Offer

 Now that the property is listed, you can direct your efforts to properly exposing the property to the market, finding a buyer, and obtaining court confirmation of the sale, if necessary.

Exposing the Property

This exposure should include all the forms you are familiar with, such as preview/walk through, open houses, private showings, newspaper advertisements, and multiple listing.

The attorney will ask you what steps you have taken to expose the property, so keep track of your activities, i.e., three open houses, advertised the property for two weeks in *The Daily Times*, received three unacceptable offers, etc. An explanation of the ways in which the property was exposed will be set out in the Report of Sale and Petition for Order Confirming Sale of Real Property, so the attorney needs to know what efforts have been made to market the property. You can further expedite the sale procedure if you give the attorney the exposure information when you send him a copy of the deposit receipt. Be very specific in your description.

The Deposit Receipt

You've exposed the property and finally you have a buyer (considered a "bidder" until the court has confirmed the sale). The deposit receipt can now be signed.

Since the types of deposit receipts vary from office to office, only the provisions applicable to a probate sale are addressed here. Here are the important items to take into consideration:

Special Wording.

In the "Miscellaneous Section" of your deposit receipt, write in that "the sale is subject to confirmation of court." (See Form 6 at the end of this chapter.) If the sale takes place under IAEA, write "subject to consent of all heirs or beneficiaries, or subject to court confirmation."

Amount Bid.

Check to make sure that the amount bid (sales price) is 90% of the court appraised value. (See Chapter 3 and the local court rules in the appendix.) Otherwise, the court will not confirm the sale.

Deposit Check.

The deposit check should be a cashier's check for at least 10%. Make the check payable to the personal representative. It should read:

   [name]   , [executor/administrator] of the Estate of   [name of decedent]   , Deceased.

In many sales, 10% of the purchase price is a sizable sum. Some prospective buyers may be reluctant to tie up so much of their money while waiting for the hearing on court confirmation. They must face the fact that they could be overbid in court and lose the sale.

It will help to allay their concerns if you can tell them that the personal representative will keep the deposit in a separate, interest-bearing account and that, in the event there is a successful overbid at court and the deposit is returned to them, they will also receive the interest. You may want to add the following wording to the deposit receipt:

Cash deposit to be placed in a separate interest-bearing account. In the event this sale is not consummated because of a successful over-bid in court, principal and accrued interest to be returned to the unsuccessful bidder named herein.

For good cause, the court may be lenient on the amount of cash to accompany the bid, i.e., all cash financing by the Veterans Administration, CalVet, or other governmental agency.

If you have a situation where the cash to accompany the bid will be less than that required, tell the attorney for the representative *before* the attorney prepares the report of sale and petition for confirmation so that the appropriate language can be inserted in the petition.

Don't Open Escrow Yet.

Do not open escrow until after the court has confirmed the sale. There are several reasons why you should wait:

- In case of a successful overbid you will not have to cancel the escrow and incur any escrow charges.

- The court must confirm the terms of the sale. If you wait until after the sale is confirmed, you will open the escrow with the correct terms and unnecessary amendments can be avoided. The escrow procedure will run smoother and more expeditiously.

Report of Sale and Petition for Order Confirming Sale of Real Property (When Court Confirmation Required)

When you have a signed deposit receipt (called a bid until the court confirms the sale) indicating an offer to purchase the property, immediately send a copy of the deposit receipt, along with a copy of the listing agreement (if you have not already done so), to the attorney for the representative. The attorney will then prepare the Report of Sale and Petition for Order Confirming Sale of Real Property to present the offer to the court. (See Form 7 at the end of this chapter.)

The report of sale and petition for order confirming sale must be filed within 30 days after the date of acceptance of a contract in a private sale. (Probate Code Section 10308.)

If, for whatever reason, the personal representative fails to file the report of sale and petition within 30 days, the purchaser may file the petition, so that the sale is not lost. (Probate Code Section 10308[b].) In this instance, the buyer may want to retain an attorney to prepare and file the petition.

Ordinarily the court will not confirm a sale where the buyer assumes an existing encumbrance, which would leave the estate subject to a contingent liability. For example, if a buyer assumes a mortgage and then defaults, the liability might go back to the estate, or to the heirs if the estate has been distributed. The executor or administrator might be held personally liable if the heirs decided to sue. The estate and the court wish to avoid such a situation, and prefer a clean-cut sale. The report and petition should set forth all pertinent facts so that the court can make a determination.

If, under the provisions of the Will, the property being sold has been given specifically to an individual(s), a 10-day notice of the report and petition for confirmation of sale must be given or the consent of the individual(s) obtained to the sale. Some counties require that this is done even before the property is offered for sale, or that consent of the individuals is on file before the hearing. (See the appendix for local court rules.)

Ask the attorney to send you a copy of the petition and notify you of the hearing date so that you and the buyer(s) can be present.

The Court Confirmation Hearing

The attorney and the representative will be in court to act on any overbids. If the attorney for the personal representative is absent from the hearing, the court may continue the hearing to another date or drop the matter completely (this varies from county to county — check the appendix for local court rules). The bidder or the bidder's representative or broker should, of course, attend the hearing. The listing agent should also attend.

Any individual interested in making an overbid on the property should attend the hearing, accompanied by his or her broker, if represented by a broker. The potential overbidder

needs to bring a cashier's check or cash for 10% of the overbid.

Bidding Procedure.

The judge or the attorney will summarize the description of the property and terms of sale and then entertain any overbids. Any discrepancies in the petition will be cleared up before the overbid procedure commences. The first overbid must exceed the original bid by 10% of the first $10,000 and 5% of the excess. (Probate Code Section 10311.)

Example:

Original bid	$200,000
First overbid must be:	
$10,000 x 10% =	$1,000
$190,000 x 5% =	9,500
Total	10,500
Add original bid	200,000
First overbid must be:	210,500

If there are no overbids and the report of sale and petition is in order, the court will confirm the sale to the original bidder. If there is bidding, the successful overbidder must file a written bid with the court. The form of written bid will vary with the court. Be sure the attorney has sufficient information to fill out the form. (See Form 8 at the end of this chapter.)

Once the original bid has been overbid in court, the original bidder may elect to be represented by a broker in further bidding, or represent himself if he doesn't have a broker.

So that you will be at ease at the hearing, the following is an outline of the procedures. Let's assume that the property in question is located at 10 Best Place, Heavenly, California. The listing broker is Broker A, with an exclusive listing. The original bidder is represented by Broker B. There are two overbidders, represented by brokers C and D.

The court will give the name of the estate and the address and legal description of the property. The court will then ask if anyone in court is interested in bidding on 10 Best Place, Heavenly, California. The minimum overbid will be stated. Anyone interested should step forward. The court will ask your name and the name of the party you represent. Stand with your client and remember that everything you say will be taken down by a court reporter, so wait your turn and don't speak out over other bidders.

The court will set the increments that the bidding should proceed at ($500, $1,000, $2,000, $5,000, for example). You may bid more, but not less than the amount set by the court.

Often there will be several bidders and the judge will determine the order of bidding.

The dialogue usually goes something like the following:

The court: *Is there anyone here who wants to bid on 10 Best Place? The minimum overbid is $210,500.*

Broker C: *Yes, Your Honor.*

Broker D: *Yes, Your Honor.*

Court: *Is the original bidder in court?*

Broker B: *Yes, Your Honor.*

Court: *Would everyone interested please come forward and state your names for the record.*

I am Broker A and I am the listing broker.

I am Broker B and I represent the original bidder.

I am Broker C and I represent an overbidder.

I am Broker D and I represent an overbidder.

Court: *Do you understand that this is an "as is" sale?*

Broker C: *Yes, Your Honor.*

Broker D: *Yes, Your Honor.*

Court: *Do you each have a cashier's check or cash for 10% of the overbid?*

Broker C: *Yes.*

Broker D: *Yes.*

(Broker B, representing the original bidder, has already provided a deposit.)

Court: *Bidding will proceed in increments of $1,000, starting with Broker C.*

Broker C: *$210,500.*

Broker D: *$211,500.*
Broker B: *$212,500.*
Bidding proceeds until all but one, the original bidder, has dropped out.

Court: *The court hereby confirms the sale of the real property located at 10 Best Place, Heavenly, California, to the original bidder, for $215,500.*

The commission of $12,930.00 is ordered, payable one-half or the sum of $6,465 to Broker A, the listing broker with an exclusive listing; and one-half or the sum of $6,465 to Broker B, the broker for the original bidder. The attorney will submit an order to this court showing the division of commissions.

Credit Overbids.

Credit overbids present a question as to whether the amount offered on the terms presented is the best bid. While the court is obliged to confirm the highest and best bid, if an overbid is upon credit, the overbid will only be considered by the court if the personal representative or his or her attorney informs the court that the bid is acceptable. The court must consider not only whether the bid is arithmetically the highest, but also whether it is best. The attorney or the parties involved should be prepared with factual information that will aid the court in making the determination. (Probate Code Section 10311[d].)

If the bid returned for confirmation is:

1. Upon credit, and a higher offer is made to the court, either for cash or upon credit,

whether on the same or different credit terms, or;

    2. For cash and a higher offer made to the court is upon credit;

the offer will be considered only if the personal representative informs the court that the offer is acceptable prior to confirmation of the sale.

Overbids and Commissions

The decedent died during a time when the real estate market was in a slump. The real property, a lot in Apple Valley in the Southern California desert, was originally appraised for $19,000 and had been listed for sale for some time. No power of sale was specified in the Will, so a notice of intention to sell was published in the local newspapers. No offers were received.

The estate remained dormant for several years. It then became imperative that the estate close, so to expose the property another notice of intention to sell was published in the local newspapers. The notice stated that the property would be sold for "cash or such credit terms and conditions as the court may approve." Still no offers.

Finally, the executor advertised the property in a real estate magazine. In the meantime, the city had imposed a building moratorium because of sewer problems and this made it very advantageous for a building permit to be taken out before a certain date. A broker saw the ad and presented an offer on behalf of his client for $17,500, cash down of $10,000 and a note secured by a deed of trust for $7,500. The offer was accepted, subject to court confirmation, of course.

The attorney prepared the report of sale and petition for confirmation. The hearing was set for one month later. Proper notice was given to all beneficiaries.

To show you how a sale can so easily be delayed, the appraisal was more than one year old. The sale was continued so a reappraisal could be filed.

Between the advertising and the city moratorium, considerable interest was expressed in the property. Several agents called the attorney stating their clients were going to attend the hearing and overbid.

Two additional bidders appeared at the hearing. The amount required for the first overbid was $18,875.00. Since the notice stated the property could be sold for terms, the bidding went back and forth between so much down and a note for so much at so much interest. An overbidder finally offered to pay cash.

The bidding had continued late in the day, so the executor and his attorney asked that the hearing be continued again to allow them time to review the bids and see which terms were the most advantageous to the estate.

At the continued hearing two weeks later, the bidding continued until the sale was confirmed to the second overbidder at $29,500, with $17,000 cash down payment and a note secured by a deed of trust for $12,500.

The broker for the original bidder did not have an exclusive listing agreement and did not receive a commission because his bidder was unsuccessful. The successful overbidder represented himself, so no commission was paid. The broker could easily have asked the executor to sign a listing agreement so that he would have been assured a commission.

You can bet that next time that broker will ask for a listing agreement!

The Broker's Commission

A Broker Bidding for His Own Account Is Not Entitled to a Commission.

According to a legal precedent, a broker bidding for his own account is not entitled to receive or share in a commission. (Estate of Toy (1977) 72 Cal.App.3d 392.)

How to Figure the Commission.

The following are examples of how the court will fix the commission in different sets of circumstances. Also refer to the appendix for the local court rules in the county in which the report of sale and petition was filed.

At the hearing it is possible that the sale could be confirmed to an overbidder, so, if you represent the original bidder, you and the buyer(s) should be present in court because you will have an opportunity to overbid the overbidder.

There is an additional limitation on the commission of an agent or broker producing a successful overbidder. If the original bidder is not represented by a broker, but the successful overbidder is so represented, the commission to the broker who represents the overbidder shall not exceed one-half of the difference between the amount of the original bid and the amount of the successful overbid. This limitation does not apply to a broker who holds an exclusive listing agreement. (Probate Code Section 10162.)

In the following examples:

Broker A is the listing broker, with an exclusive contract;

Broker B is the broker for the original bidder;

Broker C is the broker for a successful overbidder.

There's an exclusive listing and the sale is confirmed to the original bidder.

Example 1. Broker A, with an exclusive contract, produces the original bid which is confirmed by the court: the court will fix the commission to Broker A based on local court rules, but shall not exceed the amount provided in the contract. (Probate Code Section 10162.5.)

Example 2. If Broker A has an exclusive listing contract and the original bidder is not represented by a broker, Broker A is allowed a commission on the amount for which the sale is confirmed. (Probate Code Section 10162.5.)

Example 3. Broker A has an exclusive listing contract; the original bidder is represented by Broker B: absent an agreement, Broker A and Broker B divide the commission equally based on the amount of the original bid. (Probate Code Section 10162.7.)

The court would prefer that the exclusive listing broker and the broker for the buyer(s) enter into an agreement for the division of the commission rather than requiring the court to decide the division at the time of the confirmation hearing.

There's an exclusive listing and the sale is confirmed to a successful overbidder.

Example 4. Broker A with an exclusive contract produces the original bid; a successful overbidder is not represented by a broker: the court shall allow a commission on the amount of the original bid, based on local court rules, to Broker A. (Probate Code Section 10162.5.)

Example 5. Broker A has an exclusive listing contract; original bid produced by Broker B; successful overbid by purchaser not represented by broker: reasonable commission on amount of original bid, absent an agreement, divided equally between Broker A and Broker B. (Probate Code Section 10164[c].)

Example 6. Broker A with exclusive listing produces original bidder; successful overbidder represented by Broker C: the commission is divided as follows:

One-half of commission on original bid to Broker A;

One-half of commission on original bid plus all on overbid to Broker C. (Probate Code Section 10165[c][1].)

For example, Broker A returns a $200,000 bid for confirmation, and Broker C brings in an increased bid of $210,500 on which the sale is confirmed. The court awards 6% of $210,500 or $12,630 in commissions. Broker A receives one-half of the commission on the original bid ($200,000 at 6% commission equals $12,000; one-half of $12,000 equals $6,000) or $6,000. Broker C receives the other one-half of the commission on the original bid ($6,000) plus all of the commission on the amount of the difference between the original bid and the amount for which the sale is confirmed (6% of the difference between $210,500 and $200,000 or $630). Broker C thus receives $6,630.

Example 7. Broker A has exclusive listing contract; original bid produced by Broker B; successful overbid by purchaser represented by Broker C: Broker A and Broker B share one-half of the commission on the original bid equally, unless otherwise provided in an agreement between them. (Probate Code Section 10165.)

Broker C receives one-half of the commission on the original bid plus all of the commission on the overbid.

For example, Broker B returns a $200,000 bid for confirmation and Broker C brings in an increased bid of $210,500 on which the sale is confirmed. The court awards 6% of $210,500 or $12,630 in commissions. Broker A (holder of exclusive sales contract) and Broker B (broker producing purchaser whose bid was returned to the court for confirmation) are entitled to share one-half of the commission on the original bid or $6,000 ($200,000 at 6% commission equals $12,000, one-half of $12,000 equals $6,000). The one-half commission on the original bid ($6,000) is divided equally between Brokers A and B (each receiving $3,000), unless otherwise provided in an agreement between them. Broker C receives the other one-half of the commission on the original bid ($6,000) plus all of the commission on the amount of the difference between the original bid and the amount for which the sale is confirmed (6% of the difference between $210,500 and $200,000 or $630). Broker C thus receives $6,630.

Example 8. Broker A has exclusive listing contract; bidder whose bid is returned to court not represented by a broker; successful overbidder not represented by a broker: Broker A is allowed a commission which the court determines is reasonable, based on the amount of the original bid. (Probate Code Section 10162.5[b].)

There's no exclusive listing and the sale is confirmed to the original bidder.

Example 9. If there's no Broker A or Broker A does not have an exclusive listing and Broker B produces a bid returned to court, Broker B is allowed a commission on the amount for which the sale is confirmed. (Probate Code Section 10162.3.)

There's no exclusive listing and the sale is confirmed to a successful overbidder.

Example 10. No listing broker (no Broker A); original bidder not represented by broker

(no Broker B); successful overbidder represented by Broker C: reasonable commission on
full amount for which sale confirmed payable
to Broker C, subject to limitation that it may
not exceed one-half of the difference between
the amount of the original bid and the amount
of the successful overbid. (Probate Code Section 10163.)

Example 11. The original bidder is represented by Broker B. The successful overbidder
has no broker. Broker B gets the entire commission, based on the original bid. (Probate
Code Section 10164[a][b].)

Example 12. The original bidder is represented by Broker B; the successful overbidder
is represented by Broker C. Broker B gets 50%
of the commission based on the original bid.
Broker C gets the other 50% of the commission
based on the original bid, plus 100% of the
commission on the difference between the
original and successful bids. (Probate Code
Section 10165[c][2].)

Postponement of the Hearing
Can Cause a Domino Effect

Most real estate sales resemble a line of delicately poised dominoes, with buyers and sellers down the line trying to time the close of their escrows to fit each others' plans. One problem can cause the dominoes to fall, affecting people who aren't even directly connected in a sale. Probate sales are even more so, with the additional requirements and the potential for the original bidder to be overbid in court and lose the purchase.

In such a situation, a broker represented an executor who was selling estate property. At the court confirmation hearing, the potential buyer of the estate property was very nervous because she had sold her house contingent upon the court confirming the sale.

The court commissioner continued the hearing for three weeks because the appraisal was more than one year old, by a few days. If you recall, the Probate Code (Section 10309) states that the real property must have been appraised within one year prior to the date of the hearing.

The delay caused a domino effect because the buyer of the estate property was afraid the buyer of her property would back out when she was unable to timely close her escrow. If she removed the contingency that the estate property must be confirmed before the escrow on her house could close, then she might wind up on the street without a home.

The buyer of the estate property threatened to sue because of the error. She had made plans thinking the escrow on the estate property would close.

The commissioner understood the problem and moved the hearing up on the court calendar. The sale was confirmed.

Remember, though, that the executor is under no obligation to complete the sale until it is confirmed by the court. A probate sale is not a sure thing until then, because an overbid in court can wipe out the original bid.

An estate sale often presents hard choices for a buyer who is at the same time selling his or her house because the buyer must complete the obligation of selling that home, even if he or she loses out on the estate sale by an overbid. The risk of being without a place to live looms large.

Note that in this case there were two different escrows and four different parties: the escrow on estate property and the escrow on the buyer's house, the sale of which was contingent upon the estate escrow closing. The four parties were the estate, the buyer of estate property also functioning as the seller of her house, and the buyer of her house.

You can see that, with these complications, it's wise to make sure all the steps, such as the timing of the appraisal, have been properly completed before you go into court.

REAL ESTATE PURCHASE CONTRACT AND RECEIPT FOR DEPOSIT
THIS IS MORE THAN A RECEIPT FOR MONEY. IT IS INTENDED TO BE A LEGALLY-BINDING CONTRACT. READ IT CAREFULLY.
CALIFORNIA ASSOCIATION OF REALTORS' (CAR) STANDARD FORM

_____ Heavenly _____, California. _____ October 15 _____, 19 89

Received from __ Bill and Betty Buyer _____

herein called Buyer, the sum of ____ One Thousand _____ Dollars $ 1,000.00

evidenced by ☐ cash, ☒ cashier's check, ☐ personal check or ☐ _____ -- _____, payable to Decade 40 Real Estate
_____, to be held uncashed until acceptance of this offer as deposit on account of purchase price of

____ Two Hundred Thousand _____ Dollars $ 200,000.00

for the purchase of property, situated in _____ City of Heavenly _____, County of _____ Comfort _____, California.

described as follows: 10 Best Place, Heavenly, CA, Lot 101, Block 5, Heavenly Ranchos

1. FINANCING: The obtaining of Buyer's financing is a contingency of this agreement.

  A. DEPOSIT upon acceptance, to be deposited into First American Title, Escrow Division _____ $ 1,000.00

  B. INCREASED DEPOSIT within _____ days of acceptance to be deposited into _____ $

  C. BALANCE OF DOWN PAYMENT to be deposited into escrow ___ on or before close of escrow $ 19,000.00 $ 180,000.00

  D. Buyer to apply, qualify for and obtain a NEW FIRST LOAN in the amount of . . . .

    payable monthly at approximately $ 2,000.00 including interest at origination not to exceed 10 %.

    ☐ fixed rate, ☐ other _____ all due 30 years from date of origination. Loan fee not to

    exceed _____. Seller agrees to pay a maximum of _____ FHA/VA discount points.

    Additional terms _____

  _____

  E. Buyer ☐ to assume, ☐ to take title subject to an EXISTING FIRST LOAN with an approximate balance of . . . . $ --

    in favor of _____ payable monthly at $ _____ including interest at _____ % ☐ fixed rate,

    ☐ other _____. Fees not to exceed _____.

    Disposition of impound account _____

    Additional terms _____

  F. Buyer to execute a NOTE SECURED BY a ☐ first, ☐ second, ☐ third DEED OF TRUST in the amount of . . . . $ --

    IN FAVOR OF SELLER payable monthly at $ _____ ☐ or more, including interest at _____ % all due

    _____ years from date of origination, ☐ or upon sale or transfer of subject property. A late charge of _____

    _____ shall be due on any installment not paid within _____ days of the due date.

    ☐ Deed of Trust to contain a request for notice of default or sale for the benefit of Seller. Buyer ☐ will, ☐ will not execute a request

    for notice of delinquency. Additional terms _____

  _____

  G. Buyer ☐ to assume, ☐ to take title subject to an EXISTING SECOND LOAN with an approximate balance of . . . . $ --

    in favor of _____ payable monthly at $ _____ including interest at _____ %

    ☐ fixed rate, ☐ other _____. Buyer fees not to exceed _____

    Additional terms _____

  _____

H. Buyer to apply, qualify for and obtain a NEW SECOND LOAN in the amount of . . . . $ ___
payable monthly at approximately $_____ including interest at origination not to exceed _____% ☐ fixed rate,
☐ other _____ , all due _____ years from date of origination.
Buyer's loan fee not to exceed _____ . Additional terms _____

I. In the event Buyer assumes or takes title subject to an existing loan, Seller shall provide Buyer with copies of applicable notes and Deeds of Trust. A loan may contain a number of features which affect the loan, such as interest rate changes, monthly payment changes, balloon payments, etc. Buyer shall be allowed _____ calendar days after receipt of such copies to notify Seller in writing of disapproval. FAILURE TO NOTIFY SELLER IN WRITING SHALL CONCLUSIVELY BE CONSIDERED APPROVAL. Buyer's approval shall not be unreasonably withheld. Difference in existing loan balances shall be adjusted in ☐ Cash, ☐ Other _____

J. Buyer agrees to act diligently and in good faith to obtain all applicable financing. _____

K. ADDITIONAL FINANCING TERMS: _____

L. TOTAL PURCHASE PRICE . . . . $ 200,000.00

2. **OCCUPANCY:** Buyer ☒ does, ☐ does not intend to occupy subject property as Buyer's primary residence.

3. **SUPPLEMENTS:** The ATTACHED supplements are incorporated herein:
☐ Interim Occupancy Agreement (CAR FORM I0A-11)   ☐ ___
☐ Residential Lease Agreement after Sale (CAR FORM RLAS-11)   ☐ ___
☐ VA and FHA Amendments (CAR FORM VA/FHA-11)   ☐ ___

4. **ESCROW:** Buyer and Seller shall deliver signed instructions to First American Title, Escrow Division the escrow holder, within 7 calendar days of acceptance of the offer which shall provide for closing within 45 calendar days of acceptance. Escrow fees to be paid as follows: 1/2 by Buyer, 1/2 by Seller

Buyer and Seller acknowledge receipt of copy of this page, which constitutes Page 1 of 4 Pages.
Buyer's Initials (BB) (BB)   Seller's Initials (IMS) ( )

THIS STANDARDIZED DOCUMENT FOR USE IN SIMPLE TRANSACTIONS HAS BEEN APPROVED BY THE CALIFORNIA ASSOCIATION OF REALTORS* IN FORM ONLY. NO REPRESENTATION IS MADE AS TO THE APPROVAL OF THE FORM OF ANY SUPPLEMENTS NOT CURRENTLY PUBLISHED BY THE CALIFORNIA ASSOCIATION OF REALTORS* OR THE LEGAL VALIDITY OR ADEQUACY OF ANY PROVISION IN ANY SPECIFIC TRANSACTION. IT SHOULD NOT BE USED IN COMPLEX TRANSACTIONS OR WITH EXTENSIVE RIDERS OR ADDITIONS.
A REAL ESTATE BROKER IS THE PERSON QUALIFIED TO ADVISE ON REAL ESTATE TRANSACTIONS. IF YOU DESIRE LEGAL OR TAX ADVICE, CONSULT AN APPROPRIATE PROFESSIONAL.

Copyright 1989, CALIFORNIA ASSOCIATION OF REALTORS*
525 South Virgil Avenue, Los Angeles, California 90020
REVISED 2/89

QUADRUPLICATE

OFFICE USE ONLY
Reviewed by Broker or Designee
Date

REAL ESTATE PURCHASE CONTRACT AND RECEIPT FOR DEPOSIT (DLF-14 PAGE 1 OF 4)

**Form 6, Page 2
Real Estate Purchase Contract and
Receipt for Deposit**

Subject Property Address: _____ 10 Heavenly Place _____

5. **TITLE:** Title is to be free of liens, encumbrances, easements, restrictions, rights and conditions of record or known to Seller, other than the following: (a) Current property taxes; (b) covenants, conditions, restrictions, and public utility easements of record, if any, provided the same do not adversely affect the continued use of the property for the purposes for which it is presently being used, unless reasonably disapproved by Buyer in writing within ____ five ____ calendar days of receipt of a current preliminary report furnished at _____ Seller's _____ expense, and (c) ____ -- ____

Seller shall furnish Buyer at _____ Seller's _____ expense a California Land Title Association policy issued by ____ FIRST ____ AMERICAN TITLE _____ Company, showing title vested in Buyer subject only to the above. If Seller is unwilling or unable to eliminate any title matter disapproved by Buyer as above, Buyer may terminate this agreement. If Seller fails to deliver title as above, Buyer may terminate this agreement; in either case, the deposit shall be returned to Buyer.

6. **VESTING:** Unless otherwise designated in the escrow instructions of Buyer, title shall vest as follows: ____ Bill Buyer and Betty Buyer, as joint tenants _____

(The manner of taking title may have significant legal and tax consequences. Therefore, give this matter serious consideration.)

7. **PRORATIONS:** Property taxes, payments on bonds and assessments assumed by Buyer, interest, rents, association dues, premiums on insurance acceptable to Buyer, and _____ -- _____ shall be paid current and prorated as of $\boxed{XX}$ the day of recordation of the deed; or ☐ _____ -- _____ . Bonds or assessments now a lien shall be $\boxed{XX}$ paid current by Seller, payments not yet due to be assumed by Buyer; or ☐ paid in full by Seller, including payments not yet due; or ☐ _____ -- _____ . County Transfer tax shall be paid by _____ Seller _____ . The _____ -- _____ transfer tax or transfer fee shall be paid by _____ Seller _____ . **PROPERTY WILL BE REASSESSED UPON CHANGE OF OWNERSHIP. THIS WILL AFFECT THE TAXES TO BE PAID.** A Supplemental tax bill will be issued, which shall be paid as follows: (a) for periods after close of escrow, by Buyer (or by final acquiring party if part of an exchange), and (b) for periods prior to close of escrow, by Seller. TAX BILLS ISSUED AFTER CLOSE OF ESCROW SHALL BE HANDLED DIRECTLY BETWEEN BUYER AND SELLER.

8. **POSSESSION:** Possession and occupancy shall be delivered to Buyer, ☐ on close of escrow, or $\boxed{X}$ not later than ____ 3 ____ days after close of escrow, or ☐ _____ -- _____ .

9. **KEYS:** Seller shall, when possession is available to Buyer, provide keys and/or means to operate all property locks, and alarms, if any.

10. **PERSONAL PROPERTY:** The following items of personal property, free of liens and without warranty of condition, are included: ____ none ____

11. **FIXTURES:** All permanently installed fixtures and fittings that are attached to the property or for which special openings have been made are included in the purchase price, including electrical, light, plumbing and heating fixtures, built-in appliances, screens, awnings, shutters, all window coverings, attached floor coverings, TV antennas, air cooler or conditioner, garage door openers and controls, attached fireplace equipment, mailbox, trees and shrubs, and _____ -- _____ except _____ -- _____ .

12. **SMOKE DETECTOR(S):** State law requires that residences be equipped with an operable smoke detector(s). Local law may have additional requirements. Seller shall deliver to Buyer a written statement of compliance in accordance with applicable state and local law prior to close of escrow.

13. **TRANSFER DISCLOSURE:** Unless exempt, Transferor (Seller), shall comply with Civil Code §§1102 et seq., by providing Transferee (Buyer) with a Real Estate Transfer Disclosure Statement: (a) ☐ Buyer has received and read a Real Estate Transfer Disclosure Statement; or (b) $\boxed{x}$ Seller shall provide Buyer with a Real Estate Transfer Disclosure Statement within ____ 5 ____ calendar days of acceptance of the offer after which Buyer shall have three (3) days after delivery to Buyer, in person, or five (5) days after delivery by deposit in the mail, to terminate this agreement by delivery of a written notice of termination to Seller or Seller's Agent,

Form 6, Page 3
Real Estate Purchase Contract and
Receipt for Deposit

14. TAX WITHHOLDING: Under the Foreign Investment in Real Property Tax Act (FIRPTA), IRC §1445, *every* Buyer of U.S. real property *must,* unless an exemption applies, deduct and withhold from Seller's proceeds 10% of the gross sales price. Under California Revenue and Taxation Code §§18805 and 26131, the Buyer must deduct and withhold an additional one-third of the amount required to be withheld under federal law. The primary FIRPTA exemptions are: No withholding is required if (a) Seller provides Buyer with an affidavit under penalty of perjury, that Seller is not a "foreign person," or (b) Seller provides Buyer with a "qualifying statement" issued by the Internal Revenue Service, or (c) Buyer purchases real property for use as a residence and the purchase price is $300,000 or less and Buyer or a member of Buyer's family has definite plans to reside at the property for at least 50% of the number of days it is in use during each of the first two twelve-month periods after transfer. Seller and Buyer agree to execute and deliver as directed any instrument, affidavit, or statement reasonably necessary to carry out those statutes and regulations promulgated thereunder.

15. MULTIPLE LISTING SERVICE: If Broker is a Participant of an Association/Board multiple listing service ("MLS"), the Broker is authorized to report the sale, its price, terms, and financing for the publication, dissemination, information, and use of the authorized Board members, MLS Participants and Subscribers.

16. ADDITIONAL TERMS AND CONDITIONS:

ONLY THE FOLLOWING PARAGRAPHS 'A' THROUGH 'K' *WHEN INITIALLED BY BOTH BUYER AND SELLER* ARE INCORPORATED IN THIS AGREEMENT.

Buyer's Initials   Seller's Initials

_____ / _____ / _____   **A. PHYSICAL AND GEOLOGICAL INSPECTION:** Buyer shall have the right, at Buyer's expense, to select a licensed contractor and/or other qualified professional(s), to make "Inspections" (including tests, surveys, other studies, inspections, and investigations) of the subject property, including but not limited to structural, plumbing, sewer/septic system, well, heating, electrical, built-in appliances, roof, soils, foundation, mechanical systems, pool, pool heater, pool filter, air conditioner, if any, possible environmental hazards such as asbestos, formaldehyde, radon gas and other substances/products, and geologic conditions. Buyer shall keep the subject property free and clear of any liens, indemnify and hold Seller harmless from all liability, claims, demands, damages, or costs, and repair all damages to the property arising from the "Inspections." All claimed defects concerning the condition of the property that adversely affect the continued use of the property for the purposes for which it is presently being used (☐ or as _____) shall be in writing, supported by written reports, if any, and delivered to Seller within _____ calendar days FOR "INSPECTIONS" OTHER THAN GEOLOGICAL, and/or within _____ calendar days FOR GEOLOGICAL "INSPECTIONS," **of acceptance of the offer.** Buyer shall furnish Seller copies, at no cost, of all reports concerning the property obtained by Buyer. When such reports disclose conditions or information unsatisfactory to the Buyer, which the Seller is unwilling or unable to correct, Buyer may cancel this agreement. Seller shall make the premises available for all Inspections. BUYER'S FAILURE TO NOTIFY SELLER IN WRITING SHALL CONCLUSIVELY BE CONSIDERED APPROVAL.

Buyer's Initials   Seller's Initials

BB/BB   IMS/   **B. CONDITION OF PROPERTY:** Seller warrants, through the date possession is made available to Buyer: (1) property and improvements, including landscaping, grounds and pool/spa, if any, shall be maintained in the same condition as upon the date of acceptance of the offer, and (2) the roof is free of all known leaks, and (3) built-in appliances, and water, sewer/septic, plumbing, heating, electrical, air conditioning, pool/spa systems, if any, are operative, and (4) Seller shall replace all broken and/or cracked glass; (5) _____.

Buyer's Initials   Seller's Initials

BB/ BB   IMS/   **C. SELLER REPRESENTATION:** Seller warrants that Seller has no knowledge of any notice of violations of City, County, State, Federal, Building, Zoning, Fire, Health Codes or ordinances, or other governmental regulation filed or issued against the property. This warranty shall be effective until the date of close of escrow.

Buyer and Seller acknowledge receipt of copy of this page, which constitutes Page 2 of ___4___ Pages.

Buyer's Initials (BB) (BB) Seller's Initials (IMS) (_____)

┌─ OFFICE USE ONLY ─┐
Reviewed by Broker or Designee _____
Date _____

QUADRUPLICATE

EQUAL HOUSING OPPORTUNITY
M-SF-Aug-89

REAL ESTATE PURCHASE CONTRACT AND RECEIPT FOR DEPOSIT (DLF-14 PAGE 2 OF 4)

**Form 6, Page 4
Real Estate Purchase Contract and
Receipt for Deposit**

Subject Property Address _____ 10 Heavenly Place _____

Buyer's Initials   Seller's Initials
____ / ____   ____ / ____   **D. PEST CONTROL:** (1) Within _____ calendar days of acceptance of the offer, Seller shall furnish Buyer at the expense of ☐ Buyer, ☐ Seller, a current written report of an inspection by _____ . a licensed Structural Pest Control Operator, of the main building, ☐ detached garage(s) or carport(s), if any, and ☐ the following other structures on the property:
_____

(2) If requested by either Buyer or Seller, the report shall separately identify each recommendation for corrective measures as follows:

"Section 1": Infestation or infection which is evident.

"Section 2": Conditions that are present which are deemed likely to lead to infestation or infection.

(3) If no infestation or infection by wood destroying pests or organisms is found, the report shall include a written Certification as provided in Business and Professions Code § 8519(a) that on the date of inspection "no evidence of active infestation or infection was found."

(4) All work recommended to correct conditions described in "Section 1" shall be at the expense of ☐ Buyer, ☐ Seller.

(5) All work recommended to correct conditions described in "Section 2," if requested by Buyer, shall be at the expense of ☐ Buyer, ☐ Seller.

(6) The repairs shall be performed with good workmanship and materials of comparable quality and shall include repairs of leaking showers, replacement of tiles and other materials removed for repairs. It is understood that exact restoration of appearance or cosmetic items following all such repairs is not included.

(7) Funds for work agreed to be performed after close of escrow, shall be held in escrow and disbursed upon receipt of a written Certification as provided in Business and Professions Code § 8519(b) that the inspected property "is now free of evidence of active infestation or infection."

(8) Work to be performed at Seller's expense may be performed by Seller or through others, provided that (a) all required permits and final inspections are obtained, and (b) upon completion of repairs a written Certification is issued by a licensed Structural Pest Control Operator showing that the inspected property "is now free of evidence of active infestation or infection."

(9) If inspection of inaccessible areas is recommended by the report, Buyer has the option to accept and approve the report, or within _____ calendar days from receipt of the report to request in writing further inspection be made. BUYER'S FAILURE TO NOTIFY SELLER IN WRITING OF SUCH REQUEST SHALL CONCLUSIVELY BE CONSIDERED APPROVAL OF THE REPORT. If further inspection recommends "Section 1" and/or "Section 2" corrective measures, such work shall be at the expense of the party designated in subparagraph (4) and/or (5), respectively. If no infestation or infection is found, the cost of inspection, entry and closing of the inaccessible areas shall be at the expense of the Buyer.

(10) Other _____
_____

Buyer's Initials   Seller's Initials
____ / ____   ____ / ____   **E. FLOOD HAZARD AREA DISCLOSURE:** Buyer is informed that subject property is situated in a "Special Flood Hazard Area" as set forth on a Federal Emergency Management Agency (FEMA) "Flood Insurance Rate Map" (FIRM), or "Flood Hazard Boundary Map" (FHBM). The law provides that, as a condition of obtaining financing on most structures located in a "Special Flood Hazard Area," lenders require flood insurance where the property or its attachments are security for a loan.

The extent of coverage and the cost may vary. For further information consult the lender or insurance carrier. No representation or recommendation is made by the Seller and the Broker(s) in this transaction as to the legal effect or economic consequences of the National Flood Insurance Program and related legislation.

Buyer's Initials   Seller's Initials
____ / ____   ____ / ____   **F. SPECIAL STUDIES ZONE DISCLOSURE:** Buyer is informed that subject property is situated in a Special Studies Zone as designated under §§ 2621-2625, inclusive, of the California Public Resources Code; and, as such, the construction or development on this property of any structure for human occupancy may be subject to the findings of a geologic report prepared by a geologist registered in the State of California, unless such a report is waived by the City or County under the terms of that act.

Form 6, Page 5
Real Estate Purchase Contract and
Receipt for Deposit

Buyer is allowed _____ calendar days from acceptance of the offer to make further inquiries at appropriate governmental agencies concerning the use of the subject property under the terms of the Special Studies Zone Act and local building, zoning, fire, health, and safety codes. When such inquiries disclose conditions or information unsatisfactory to the Buyer, which the Seller is unwilling or unable to correct, Buyer may cancel this agreement. BUYER'S FAILURE TO NOTIFY SELLER IN WRITING SHALL CONCLUSIVELY BE CONSIDERED APPROVAL.

Buyer's Initials _____ / _____ **Seller's Initials** _____ / _____

G. ENERGY CONSERVATION RETROFIT: If local ordinance requires that the property be brought in compliance with minimum energy Conservation Standards as a condition of sale or transfer, ☐ Buyer, ☐ Seller shall comply with and pay for these requirements. Where permitted by law, Seller may, if obligated hereunder, satisfy the obligation by authorizing escrow to credit Buyer with sufficient funds to cover the cost of such retrofit.

Buyer's Initials BB / BB **Seller's Initials** IMS / _____

H. HOME PROTECTION PLAN: Buyer and Seller have been informed that Home Protection Plans are available. Such plans may provide additional protection and benefit to a Seller or Buyer. The CALIFORNIA ASSOCIATION OF REALTORS® and the Broker(s) in this transaction do not endorse or approve any particular company or program:

a) ☐ A Buyer's coverage Home Protection Plan to be issued by _____
Company, at a cost not to exceed $_____ , to be paid by ☐ Buyer, ☐ Seller; or

b) ☐ Buyer and Seller elect not to purchase a Home Protection Plan.

Buyer's Initials _____ / _____ **Seller's Initials** _____ / _____

I. CONDOMINIUM/P.U.D.: The subject of this transaction is a condominium/planned unit development (P.U.D.) designated as unit _____ and _____ parking space(s) and an undivided interest in community areas, and _____ . The current monthly assessment charge by the homeowner's association or other governing body(s) is $_____ . As soon as practicable, Seller shall provide Buyer with copies of covenants, conditions and restrictions, articles of incorporation, by-laws, current rules and regulations, most current financial statements, and any other documents as required by law. Seller shall disclose in writing any known pending special assessment, claims, or litigation to Buyer. Buyer shall be allowed _____ calendar days from receipt to review these documents. If such documents disclose conditions or information unsatisfactory to Buyer, Buyer may cancel this agreement. BUYER'S FAILURE TO NOTIFY SELLER IN WRITING SHALL CONCLUSIVELY BE CONSIDERED APPROVAL.

Buyer's Initials _____ / _____ **Seller's Initials** _____ / _____

J. LIQUIDATED DAMAGES: If Buyer fails to complete said purchase as herein provided by reason of any default of Buyer, Seller shall be released from obligation to sell the property to Buyer and may proceed against Buyer upon any claim or remedy which he/she may have in law or equity; provided, however, that by initialling this paragraph Buyer and Seller agree that Seller shall retain the deposit as liquidated damages. If the described property is a dwelling with no more than four units, one of which the Buyer intends to occupy as his/her residence, Seller shall retain as liquidated damages the deposit actually paid, or an amount therefrom, not more than 3% of the purchase price and promptly return any excess to Buyer. Buyer and Seller agree to execute a similar liquidated damages provision, such as CALIFORNIA ASSOCIATION OF REALTORS® Receipt for Increased Deposit (RID-11), for any increased deposits. (Funds deposited in trust accounts or in escrow are not released automatically in the event of a dispute. Release of funds requires written agreement of the parties, judicial decision or arbitration.)

Buyer and Seller acknowledge receipt of copy of this page, which constitutes Page 3 of __4__ Pages.
Buyer's Initials (__BB__) (__BB__) Seller's Initials (__IMS__) (_____)

QUADRUPLICATE

OFFICE USE ONLY
Reviewed by Broker or Designee _____
Date _____

EQUAL HOUSING OPPORTUNITY
M–SF-Aug-89

REAL ESTATE PURCHASE CONTRACT AND RECEIPT FOR DEPOSIT (DLF-14 PAGE 3 OF 4)

**Form 6, Page 6
Real Estate Purchase Contract and
Receipt for Deposit**

Subject Property Address _____ 10 Heavenly Place _____

K. ARBITRATION OF DISPUTES: Any dispute or claim in law or equity arising out of this contract or any resulting transaction shall be decided by neutral binding arbitration in accordance with the rules of the American Arbitration Association, and not by court action except as provided by California law for judicial review of arbitration proceedings. Judgment upon the award rendered by the arbitrator(s) may be entered in any court having jurisdiction thereof. The parties shall have the right to discovery in accordance with Code of Civil Procedure § 1283.05. The following matters are excluded from arbitration hereunder: (a) a judicial or non-judicial foreclosure or other action or proceeding to enforce a deed of trust, mortgage, or real property sales contract as defined in Civil Code § 2985, (b) an unlawful detainer action, (c) the filing or enforcement of a mechanic's lien, (d) any matter which is within the jurisdiction of a probate court, or (e) an action for bodily injury or wrongful death, or for latent or patent defects to which Code of Civil Procedure § 337.1 or § 337.15 applies. The filing of a judicial action to enable the recording of a notice of pending action, for order of attachment, receivership, injunction, or other provisional remedies, shall not constitute a waiver of the right to arbitrate under this provision.

Any dispute or claim by or against broker(s) and/or associate licensee(s) participating in this transaction shall be submitted to arbitration consistent with the provision above only if the broker(s) and/or associate licensee(s) making the claim or against whom the claim is made shall have agreed to submit it to arbitration consistent with this provision.

"NOTICE: BY INITIALLING IN THE SPACE BELOW YOU ARE AGREEING TO HAVE ANY DISPUTE ARISING OUT OF THE MATTERS INCLUDED IN THE 'ARBITRATION OF DISPUTES' PROVISION DECIDED BY NEUTRAL ARBITRATION AS PROVIDED BY CALIFORNIA LAW AND YOU ARE GIVING UP ANY RIGHTS YOU MIGHT POSSESS TO HAVE THE DISPUTE LITIGATED IN A COURT OR JURY TRIAL. BY INITIALLING IN THE SPACE BELOW YOU ARE GIVING UP YOUR JUDICIAL RIGHTS TO DISCOVERY AND APPEAL, UNLESS SUCH RIGHTS ARE SPECIFICALLY INCLUDED IN THE 'ARBITRATION OF DISPUTES' PROVISION. IF YOU REFUSE TO SUBMIT TO ARBITRATION AFTER AGREEING TO THIS PROVISION, YOU MAY BE COMPELLED TO ARBITRATE UNDER THE AUTHORITY OF THE CALIFORNIA CODE OF CIVIL PROCEDURE. YOUR AGREEMENT TO THIS ARBITRATION PROVISION IS VOLUNTARY."

"WE HAVE READ AND UNDERSTAND THE FOREGOING AND AGREE TO SUBMIT DISPUTES ARISING OUT OF THE MATTERS INCLUDED IN THE 'ARBITRATION OF DISPUTES' PROVISION TO NEUTRAL ARBITRATION."

Buyer's Initials   Seller's Initials
____/____   ____/____

17. **OTHER TERMS AND CONDITIONS:** Sale is subject to consent of all heirs or beneficiaries, or subject to court confirmation.

18. **ATTORNEY'S FEES:** In any action, proceeding or arbitration arising out of this agreement, the prevailing party shall be entitled to reasonable attorney's fees and costs.

19. **ENTIRE CONTRACT:** Time is of the essence. All prior agreements between the parties are incorporated in this agreement which constitutes the entire contract. Its terms are intended by the parties as a final expression of their agreement with respect to such terms as are included herein and may not be contradicted by evidence of any prior agreement or contemporaneous oral agreement. The parties further intend that this agreement constitutes the complete and exclusive statement of its terms and that no extrinsic evidence whatsoever may be introduced in any judicial or arbitration proceeding, if any, involving this agreement.

20. **CAPTIONS:** The captions in this agreement are for convenience of reference only and are not intended as part of this agreement.

21. AGENCY CONFIRMATION: The following agency relationship(s) are hereby confirmed for this transaction:

LISTING AGENT: _Decade 40 Real Estate_ is the agent of (check one):
(Print Firm Name)

☒ the Seller exclusively; or ☐ both the Buyer and Seller

SELLING AGENT: _Warm Springs Teller Real Estate_ (if not the same as Listing Agent) is the agent of (check one):
(Print Firm Name)

☒ the Buyer exclusively; or ☐ the Seller exclusively; or ☐ both the Buyer and Seller.

22. AMENDMENTS: This agreement may not be amended, modified, altered or changed in any respect whatsoever except by a further agreement in writing executed by Buyer and Seller.

23. OFFER: This constitutes an offer to purchase the described property. Unless acceptance is signed by Seller and a signed copy delivered in person, by mail, or facsimile, and received by Buyer at the address below, or by _--_ who is authorized to receive it, on behalf of Buyer, within __2__ calendar days of the date hereof, this offer shall be deemed revoked and the deposit shall be returned. Buyer has read and acknowledges receipt of a copy of this offer. This agreement and any supplement, addendum or modification relating hereto, including any photocopy or facsimile thereof, may be executed in two or more counterparts, all of which shall constitute one and the same writing.

REAL ESTATE BROKER _Warm Springs Teller R/E_   BUYER _Betty Buyer_

By _W. E. Assist_   BUYER _Bill Buyer_

Address _100 Warm Springs Boulevard_   Address _100 Moving Place_
Heavenly, CA 90000   _Heavenly, CA 90000_

Telephone _123-6000_   Telephone _123-9876_

ACCEPTANCE

The undersigned Seller accepts and agrees to sell the property on the above terms and conditions and agrees to the above confirmation of agency relationships (☐ subject to attached counter offer).

Seller agrees to pay to Broker(s) _Decade 40 Real Estate and Warm Springs Teller Real Estate_ compensation for services as follows: _3% to Decade 40 and 3% to Warm Springs Teller_

Payable: (a) On recordation of the deed or other evidence of title, or (b) if completion of sale is prevented by default of Seller, upon Seller's default, or (c) if completion of sale is prevented by default of Buyer, only if and when Seller collects damages from Buyer, by suit or otherwise, and then in an amount not less than one-half of the damages recovered, but not to exceed the above fee, after first deducting title and escrow expenses and the expenses of collection, if any. Seller shall execute and deliver an escrow instruction irrevocably assigning the compensation for service in an amount equal to the compensation agreed to above. In any action, proceeding, or arbitration between Broker(s) and Seller arising out of this agreement, the prevailing party shall be entitled to reasonable attorney's fees and costs. The undersigned has read and acknowledges receipt of a copy of this agreement and authorizes Broker(s) to deliver a signed copy to Buyer.

Date _10/15/89_ Telephone _123-4567_   SELLER _I.M. Standin, Exec/Will of_

Address _20 Responsible Lane_
Heavenly, CA 90000   SELLER _N. O. Longerhere, Deceased_

Real Estate Broker(s) agree to the foregoing.

Broker _Decade 40 Real Estate_ By _W. E. Sell_ Date _10/15/89_

Broker _Warm Springs Teller R/E_ By _W. E. Assist_ Date _10/15/89_

QUADRUPLICATE

Page 4 of __4__ Pages.

OFFICE USE ONLY
Reviewed by Broker or Designee _____
Date _____

EQUAL HOUSING OPPORTUNITY

M-SF-Aug-89

REAL ESTATE PURCHASE CONTRACT AND RECEIPT FOR DEPOSIT (DLF-14 PAGE 4 OF 4)

Form 6, Page 8
Real Estate Purchase Contract and
Receipt for Deposit

ATTORNEY OR PARTY WITHOUT ATTORNEY (Name and Address):	TELEPHONE NO.: (415) 100-1000	FOR COURT USE ONLY
JOHN Q. LAWYER 100 City Justice Building Suite 200 Heavenly, CA 90000 ATTORNEY FOR (Name): Petitioner		

SUPERIOR COURT OF CALIFORNIA, COUNTY OF COMFORT
STREET ADDRESS: Court Building
MAILING ADDRESS: Court Building
CITY AND ZIP CODE: Heavenly, CA 900000
BRANCH NAME:

ESTATE OF (NAME): N. O. LONGERHERE	CASE NO.: 10000
[X] DECEDENT ☐ CONSERVATEE ☐ MINOR	HEARING DATE:
REPORT OF SALE AND PETITION FOR ORDER CONFIRMING SALE OF REAL PROPERTY ☐ And Sale of Other Property Sold as a Unit	DEPT.: TIME:

1. Petitioner (name of each): I. M. STANDIN

    is the [X] executor   ☐ special administrator   ☐ purchaser (30 days have passed
            ☐ administrator with will annexed   ☐ conservator   since the sale - attach declaration)
            ☐ administrator   ☐ guardian
    of the estate and requests a court order for
    a. confirmation of sale of the estate's interest in the real property described in Attachment 2e.
    b. [X] confirmation of sale of the estate's interest in other property sold as a unit as described in Attachment 2c.
    c. [X] approval of commission of: 6   % in the amount of: $ 12,000   (see local court rules).
    d. additional bond ☐ is fixed at: $ [X] is not required.
2. Description of property sold
    a. Interest sold
        [X] 100% ☐ Undivided   %
    b. [X] Improved
        ☐ Unimproved
    c. ☐ Real property sold as a unit with other property (describe in Attachment 2c).
    d. Street address and location: 10 Best Place
                                    Heavenly, CA 90000
    e. Legal description is affixed as Attachment 2e (attach).
3. Appraisal
    a. Date of death of decedent or appointment of conservator or guardian: 6/1/89
    b. Appraised value at above date: $ 200,000
    c. Reappraised value within one year prior to the hearing: $ ☐ Amount includes value of other property sold
        as a unit. (If more than one year has elapsed from date 3a to the date of the hearing, reappraisal is necessary.)
    d. Appraisal or reappraisal
        [X] has been filed ☐ will be filed
4. Manner and terms of sale
    a. Name of purchaser and manner of vesting title (specify): Bill and Betty Buyer, as joint tenants

    b. ☐ Purchaser is ☐ the personal representative ☐ the attorney for the personal representative.
    c. Sale was [X] private ☐ public on (date):
    d. Amount bid: $ 200,000   Deposit: $ 20,000
    e. Payment
        [X] Cash ☐ Credit (see Attachment 4e)
    f. [X] Other terms of sale (see Attachment 4f)
    g. ☐ Mode of sale specified in will ☐ petitioner requests relief from complying for the reasons stated in Attachment 4g.
    h. ☐ Terms comply with Probate Code, § 2542 (guardianships and conservatorships only)

(Continued on reverse)

Form 7, Page 1
Report of Sale and Petition for Order
Confirming Sale of Real Property

ESTATE OF (NAME): N. O. LONGERHERE	CASE NUMBER:
	10000

5. Commission

a. ☐ Sale without broker

b. ☒ A written ☒ exclusive ☐ nonexclusive contract for commission was entered into with (name):
DECADE 40 REAL ESTATE

c. ☒ Purchaser was procured by (name): WARM SPRINGS-TELLER REAL ESTATE
a licensed real estate broker who is not buying for his or her account.

d. ☒ Commission is to be divided as follows: 3% or $6,000 to Decade 40 Real Estate
3% or $6,000 to Warm Springs-Teller Real Estate

6. Bond

a. Amount before sale: $ ☒ none

b. Additional amount needed: $ ☒ none

c. ☐ Proceeds are to be deposited in a blocked account. Receipts will be filed. (Specify institution and location):

7. Notice of sale

a. ☒ Published ☐ posted as permitted by Probate Code, § 10301 ($5,000 or less)

b. ☒ Will authorizes sale of the property

c. ☐ Will directs sale of the property

8. Notice of hearing

a. Specific devisee

  (1) ☒ None

  (2) ☐ Consent to be filed

  (3) ☐ Written notice will be given

b. Special Notice

  (1) ☒ None requested

  (2) ☐ Has been or will be waived

  (3) ☐ Required written notice will be given

c. Personal representative

  (1) ☐ Petitioner (none required)

  (2) ☐ Consent to be filed

  (3) ☐ Written notice will be given

9. Reason for sale (need not complete if 7b or 7c checked)

a. ☐ Necessary to pay

  (1) ☐ debts

  (2) ☐ devises

  (3) ☐ family allowance

  (4) ☒ expenses of administration

  (5) ☐ taxes

b. ☒ The sale is to the advantage of the estate and in the best interest of the interested persons.

10. Overbid required amount of first overbid: $ 219,500

11. Petitioner's efforts to obtain the highest and best price reasonably attainable for the property were as follows (specify activities taken to expose the property to the market, e.g., multiple listings, advertising, open houses, etc.):
The property has been listed on an Exclusive Listing Contract with Decade 40 Real Estate since September 1, 1989. Said brokers have listed the property in the multiple listing, held four open houses, advertised the property in three (3) local newspapers, have shown the property approximately ten (10) times and have received approximately seventy-five (75) telephone inquiries. The petitioner received one (1) bid.

12. ☒ Number of pages attached: one

▶ _____ ▶
(SIGNATURE OF PETITIONER*)   (SIGNATURE OF PETITIONER*)

I declare under penalty of perjury under the laws of the State of California that the foregoing is true and correct.
Date:

I. M. STANDIN . . . . ▶
(TYPE OR PRINT NAME)   (SIGNATURE OF PETITIONER*)

*All petitioners must sign the petition. Only one need sign the declaration.

DE-260, GC-060 (Rev. July 1, 1988)   REPORT OF SALE AND PETITION FOR ORDER
CONFIRMING SALE OF REAL PROPERTY
(Probate)   Page two

Form 7, Page 2
Report of Sale and Petition for Order
Confirming Sale of Real Property

SHORT TITLE: ESTATE OF N. O. LONGERHERE	CASE NUMBER:
	10000

1 Attachment 2e

2

3 Lot 101 in Block 5, as Designated on the map entitled "Heavenly

4 Ranchos, Heavenly, California", which map was filed in the office of

5 the Recorder of the County of Comfort, State of California, on

6 February 29, 1942, in Volume 26 of maps, at page 916.

7

8 Attachment 4f

9

10 TERMS OF SALE:

11 Property is sold in an "AS IS" condition.

12 Purchase price $200,000

13 Cash down   20,000

14 Balance cash   180,000 payable before close of escrow.

15

16 Taxes to be prorated as of close of escrow.

17 Seller to pay for examination of title, policy of title insurance,

18 recording of conveyance and transfer taxes.

19

20 Escrow charges to be paid 1/2 by seller and 1/2 by buyer.

21

22

23

24

25

26 *(Required for verified pleading) The items on this page stated on information and belief (specify item numbers, not line numbers):*

27 This page may be used with any Judicial Council form or any other paper filed with this court.   Page____

Form Approved by the
Judicial Council of California
MC-020 (New January 1, 1987)

ADDITIONAL PAGE
Attach to Judicial Council Form or Other Court Paper

CRC 201, 501

Form 7, Page 3
Report of Sale and Petition for Order
Confirming Sale of Real Property

BID FOR PURCHASE OF REAL PROPERTY
(Sale Requiring Probate Court Confirmation.)
CALIFORNIA ASSOCIATION OF REALTORS® (CAR) STANDARD FORM

SUPERIOR COURT OF CALIFORNIA, COUNTY OF _____ COMFORT

Estate of___ N. O. LONGERHERE _____, deceased.   Case No. ___ 10000 ___

To___ I. M. STANDIN ___, ___ Executor ___   of the ___ Will ___ of the above-named decedent
            Executor/administrator   will/estate

The undersigned hereby offer(s) the sum of $___ 210,000.00 ___
___ $21,000 down, balance of $189,000 payable at 8.75%, in monthly payments of ___
$ __1,486.89__ , which includes principal and interest (for 30 years)
                                in cash/specify credit terms

for purchase of the real property belonging to the estate of the decedent, commonly known and referred to as ___ 10 Best Place, ___
                                                                                                                      (Street address)

___ Heavenly ___, California, and more particularly described as follows: ___ Lot 101, Block 5, ___
            (City)
___ Heavenly Ranchos ___

subject to current taxes, covenants, conditions, restrictions, reservations, rights, rights-of-way, and easements of record. ~~The following encumbrance is to be assumed by the purchaser. (strike this sentence if it is not applicable)~~

Delivered to you herewith is a ☒ cashier's check ☐ other _____ in the sum of $___ 21,000 ___
being ___ 10% ___ percent of the purchase price, balance to be paid as follows: ___ on close of escrow ___
                                                                        on confirmation of the sale by the Court/(Other terms)

Rentals, taxes, expenses of operation and maintenance, and premiums on insurance acceptable to the undersigned shall be prorated as of the date of
___ recording of conveyance ___ Escrow charges, examination of title, recording of conveyance, transfer taxes and
      confirmation of sale/recording of conveyance
any title insurance shall be at the expense of the ___ in accordance with local policy ___
                                                    Seller/buyer/or other arrangements in accordance with local policy.

We have inspected the property and the offer is made as a result of this inspection, and not on any representation by the seller or any Real Estate Licensee. We agree that you offer the property without representation, warranty, or covenant of any kind, express or implied.

This sale is conditioned upon confirmation of the above-entitled Court, and shall be returned to that Court for confirmation before
___ November 30 ___, 19 __89__ , and you shall have the same set promptly for hearing. On confirmation of sale by the Court and payment of the balance of the purchase price, you shall deliver to the undersigned possession and a deed conveying all the interest belonging to the estate in the real property.

The undersigned hereby elect(s) _____ to receive title to the property in the following manner:
_____ as __ husband and wife as their community property __.
                       separate property/joint tenants/husband and wife as their community property/tenants in common

Dated___ November 15, 1989 ___   MRS. FIRST OVERBIDDER
                                            MR. FIRST OVERBIDDER
                                            (Purchaser(s))

ACCEPTANCE

Subject to confirmation of the Court, the undersigned, as _____ of the _____, of the above-
                                                          Executor/administrator   will/estate
named decedent, hereby accepts the foregoing bid of _____
_____ as purchaser(s) of all the right, title and interest
of the decedent's estate in the real property on the terms therein stated and hereby agrees to pay to _____
real estate broker, from proceeds of the sale whatever sum may be allowed by the above-entitled Court for services in securing the purchaser.

The undersigned also acknowledges receipt of a _____ check for $_____, as deposit.
                                                cashier's

Date_____
as_____ of the _____ of the above-named decedent.   Signature _____
   Executor/administrator   will/estate

ACCEPTANCE BY BROKER

The undersigned real estate broker, duly licensed by the State of California, having secured the purchaser(s) _____
_____ hereby accepts the foregoing undertaking of _____
                                                                          (Name(s))
as _____ of the _____ of the above-named decedent, to pay to the undersigned from proceeds
   Executor/administrator   will/estate
of the sale whatever sum may be allowed by the above-entitled court.
Date_____
                                                    _____
                                                    Real Estate Broker

FORM PBP-11

OFFICE USE ONLY
Reviewed by Broker or Designee_____
Date_____
SF-Apr-89

Form 8
Court Bid Form

NOTES

Chapter 6

Opening the Escrow

 Now that the court has confirmed the sale, you can open the escrow. Ask the escrow company to send the attorney for the representative a copy of the escrow instructions so that the attorney can review them for accuracy. (See Form 9-A at the end of this chapter.)

Ask the personal representative or the attorney for the representative if the supplemental tax bill has been received. As you know, in some instances property is reappraised for property tax purposes upon the death of the owner and again when the property is sold out of the estate. This results in unexpected supplemental tax bills which are in addition to the regular tax bills. The supplemental tax bill usually goes either to the representative or to the attorney for the representative.

To avoid any problem in allocating the supplemental tax between the buyer and seller, ask the escrow company to insert language in the escrow instructions to this effect:

Buyer is aware that this is a probate sale and that the death of _____ may be considered a "change of ownership" by the county tax assessor. Buyer and Seller agree that any supplemental tax bill reported to escrow holder prior to the close of escrow as a result of reappraisal by reason of such death for the fiscal year 19__19__ will be prorated in addition to the regular tax proration provided herein.

As a matter of record with which escrow holder shall have no duty or liability:

In the event such supplemental tax bill is received after the closing of this escrow, Seller will provide Buyer with a copy of the supplemental bill and a proration of the amounts payable. If the greater portion of the tax due is payable by the Seller, Buyer will forward to Seller a check payable to the Tax Collector for Buyer's portion. If the greater portion of the tax bill is payable by the Buyer, Seller will furnish Buyer with the original tax bill and a check for the estate's portion payable to the Tax Collector. Buyer and Seller mutually agree to perform the foregoing acts prior to the delinquency date stated on the supplemental tax bill.

IAEA Sale

In the event the sale is handled under the Independent Administration of Estates Act (IAEA), the following wording would be appropriate to include in the escrow instructions:

Buyer understands that the seller is authorized to sell the property pursuant to the Independent Administration of Estates Act (IAEA) contained in the California Probate Code. The closing of this escrow is subject to and conditioned upon either notice of sale being given pursuant to the provisions set forth in Section 10580 of said Code, and no objection or revocation of consent being received; or all required consents being received pursuant to Section 10582 of said Code.

In case you are wondering, Section 10580 says that a personal representative who has been granted authority to administer under this section shall give notice of proposed action prior to taking the action and Section 10582 says that notice of proposed action need not be given to any person who consents in writing to the proposed action. The consent may be executed at any time before or after the proposed action is taken.

See Form 9-B at the end of this chapter for sample escrow instructions when the property is being sold under IAEA authority.

See Chapter 2 if you have any questions regarding the Independent Administration of Estates Act.

First American Title Insurance Company

Santa Ana CALIFORNIA • TELEPHONE (714) 558-3211

ESCROW INSTRUCTIONS

BUYER

ESCROW SUMMARY	
PAID OUTSIDE ESCROW	$
CASH THROUGH ESCROW	200,000.00
ENCUMBRANCE OF RECORD	
ENCUMBRANCE OF RECORD	
PURCHASE MONEY ENCUMB.	
TOTAL CONSIDERATION	$200,000.00

Escrow Officer_____

Ref. Number _____ 12345-RF

Date   November 16, 1989

To FIRST AMERICAN TITLE INSURANCE COMPANY

I hereby agree to purchase the hereinafter described property for a total consideration of $ 200,000.00   and will on or before   January 15, 1990   hand you said consideration which is payable as follows:

$20,000.00 has been paid outside of escrow and Seller acknowledges receipt of same, the balance of $180,000.00 is to be deposited into escrow prior to close of escrow

I will deliver to you any additional funds and execute any instruments which are necessary to comply with the terms hereof, all of which you may use when you hold for me an Executors Deed executed by

I. M. STANDIN, Executor of the Estate of N. O. Longerhere, deceased

Form 9-A, Page 1
Escrow Instructions: Court Confirmation Required

and when you can issue your   Owners   coverage form policy of title insurance with
liability of $ 200,000.00   on the following described property situated in the City of   Heavenly
County of   Comfort   , State of California:

Lot 101 in Block 5, as Designated on the map entitled "Heavenly Ranchos,
Heavenly, California", which map was filed in the office of the Recorder of
the County of Comfort, State of California, on February 29, 1942, in volume 26
of maps, at page 916.

Property commomly known as: 10 Best Place, Heavenly, California 90000

showing title vested in: BILL BUYER and BETTY BUYER, husband and wife as joint tenants.

free of encumbrances except:
1.   Current   General and special taxes for fiscal year 19 90 - 19 91
2. The lien of supplemental taxes which may be assessed as a result of revised assessed values.
3. Assessments and/or Bonds
4. Covenants, conditions, restrictions, rights of way, easements, and reservations, as described in that certain preliminary title
   evidence, issued, or to be issued, herein.
5.

Closing of this escrow is subject to Confirmation of Sale by the Court and
escrow holder's receipt of a certified copy of the Order Confirming Sale of
Real Property. Escrow holder's receipt of same and the approval of First
American Title Insurance Company will be deemed the satisfaction of this
requirement.

It is understood between the parties hereto that subject property is being
purchased in its "AS IS" condition.

1039-1
(Rev. 2-86)

Form 9-A, Page 2
Escrow Instructions: Court Confirmation Required

ESCROW INSTRUCTIONS — Page 2

If instructed by the parties prorate and/or adjust the following as of   close of escrow

☒ 1. Taxes based on the amount of the last tax statement of the Tax Collector issued prior to the close of escrow. (If the amount of the new tax bill issued by the Tax Collector after close of escrow is more or less than the amount used for proration purposes, the difference, if any, will be adjusted by the parties herein outside of escrow.) Sellers are to forward to buyers any present or future tax bills on property herein.

☐ 2. Insurance (including FHA mortgage insurance, if any).

☐ 3. Interest on all existing trust deeds, improvements assessments and/or bonds taken over by buyers.

☐ 4. Rental per rent statement handed you.

☐ 5. Charge the buyer and credit the seller the amount of any funds held in an impound account, if any, in connection with an existing loan.

☐ 6. You are to hold for me   shares of water stock of the   Company.

☐ 7.

I hereby agree to pay any charges including usual buyers escrow fee and any advances and expenses that are properly chargeable to me regardless of the consummation of this escrow. At the close of escrow you are to mail all documents, checks, etc., to the person entitled thereto at the address shown in these instructions.

GENERAL PROVISIONS

1.   **Deposit of Funds & Disbursements**

You shall deposit all funds received in this escrow in any bank insured by an agency of the United States Government, including your affiliated bank, First American Trust Company, in one or more of your general escrow demand accounts. These funds may be transferred to any other general escrow demand account or accounts, in the above named bank or banks, including those maintained in your affiliated bank. All disbursements shall be made by your check. You are authorized not to close escrow or disburse until good funds have been confirmed in escrow.

2.   **Prorations and Adjustments**

The expression "close of escrow" used in this escrow means the date of which instruments referred to herein are recorded and relates only to prorations and/or adjustments unless otherwise specified.

All prorations and/or adjustments are to be made on the basis of a 30-day month unless otherwise instructed in writing.

3.   **Recordation of Instruments**

You are authorized to record any documents delivered through this escrow, the recording of which is necessary or proper in the issuance of the requested policy of title insurance.

Form 9-A, Page 3
Escrow Instructions: Court Confirmation Required

4. **Authorization to Execute Assignment of Insurance Policies**

   You are to execute on behalf of the parties hereto form assignments of interest in any insurance policies (other than title insurance) called for in this escrow; forward assignments and policies upon close of escrow to the agent with the request, first, that insurer consent to such transfer and/or attach a loss-payable clause and/or make such other additions or corrections as may have been specifically required herein, and second, that the agent thereafter forward such policies to the parties entitled to them.

   In all acts in this escrow relating to insurance, including adjustments, if any, you shall be fully protected in assuming that each policy is in force and that the necessary premium therefor has been paid.

5. **Authorization to Furnish Copies**

   You are to furnish a copy of these instructions, amendments thereto, closing statements and/or any other documents deposited in this escrow to the lender or lenders, the real estate broker or brokers and/or the attorney or attorneys involved in this transaction upon request of the lenders, brokers or attorneys.

6. **Personal Property Taxes**

   No examination or insurance as to the amount or payment of personal property taxes is required unless specifically requested.

7. **Right of Cancellation**

   Any party instructing you to cancel this escrow shall file notice of cancellation in your office, in writing. You shall within a reasonable time thereafter mail, by certified mail, one copy of the notice to each of the other parties at the addresses stated in this escrow. Unless written objection to cancellation is filed in your office by a party within ten (10) days after date of mailing, you are authorized at your option to comply with the notice an demand payment of your cancellation charges as provided in this agreement. If written objection is filed, you are authorized at your option to hold all money and instruments in this escrow and take no further action until otherwise directed, either by the parties' mutual written instructions, or final order of a court of competent jurisdiction.

8. **Action in Interpleader**

   The parties hereto expressly agree that you, as escrow holder, have the absolute right at your election to file an action in interpleader requiring the parties to answer and litigate their several claims and rights among themselves and you are authorized to deposit with the clerk of the court all documents and funds held in this escrow. In the event such action is filed, the parties jointly and severally agree to pay your cancellation charges and costs, expenses and reasonable attorney's fees which you are required to expend or incur in the interpleader action, the amount thereof to be fixed and judgment therefor to be rendered by the court. Upon the filing of the action, you shall thereupon be fully released and discharged from all obligations to further perform any duties or obligations otherwise imposed by the terms of this escrow.

9. **Termination of Agency Obligations**

   If there is no action taken on this escrow within six (6) months after the "time limit date" as set forth in the escrow instructions or written extension thereof, your agency obligation shall terminate at your option and all documents, monies or other items held by you shall be returned to the parties depositing same.

   In the event of cancellation of this escrow, whether it be at the request of any of the parties or otherwise, the fees and charges due First American Title Insurance Company, including expenditures incurred and/or authorized shall be borne equally by the parties hereto (unless otherwise agreed to specifically).

   1039-2
   (Rev. 2-80)

Form 9-A, Page 4
Escrow Instructions: Court Confirmation Required

ESCROW INSTRUCTIONS — Page 3

10. Conflicting Instructions

Should you before or after close of escrow receive or become aware of any conflicting demands or claims with respect to this escrow or the rights of any of the parties hereto, or any money or property deposited herein or affected hereby, you shall have the right to discontinue any or all further acts on your part until the conflict is resolved to your satisfaction, and you shall have the further right to commence or defend any action or proceedings for the determination of the conflict as provided in paragraphs 7 and 8 of these General Provisions.

11. Funds Retained in Escrow

If for any reason funds are retained in escrow, you may deduct therefrom __$10.00__ as a monthly charge as custodian thereof.

12. Usury

You are not to be concerned with any question of usury in any loan or encumbrances involved in the processing of this escrow and you are hereby released of any responsibility or liability therefor.

13. Indemnify for Attorneys Fees and Costs

In the event suit is brought by any party to this escrow, including the title company or any other party, as against each other, or others, including the title company, claiming any right they may have as against each other or against the title company, then in that event, the parties hereto agree to indemnify and hold harmless the title company against any attorney's fees and costs incurred by it.

14. Amendments to Escrow Instructions

Any Amendment or supplement to these escrow instructions must be in writing. These escrow instructions constitute the entire escrow between the escrow holder and the parties hereto.

15. Foreign Investment in Real Property Tax Act

The Foreign Investment in Real Property Tax Act of 1980 as amended by the Tax Reform Act of 1984 places special requirements for tax reporting and withholding on the parties to a real estate transaction where the transferor (seller) is a non-resident alien or non-domestic corporation or partnership or is a domestic corporation or partnership controlled by non-residents or non-resident corporations or partnerships. The parties to this transaction are seeking an attorney's, accountant's or other tax specialist's opinions concerning the effect of this Act on this transaction and are not acting on any statements made or omitted by the escrow or closing officer.

_____	_____
Buyer	Seller

Form 9-A, Page 5
Escrow Instructions: Court Confirmation Required

TIME IS OF THE ESSENCE OF THESE INSTRUCTIONS. If this escrow is not in condition to close by   November 30   19 89 , and demand for cancellation is received by you from any party to this escrow after said date, you shall act in accordance with the cancellation instructions contained in the general provisions on the previous page hereof. If no demand for cancellation is made, you will proceed to close this escrow when the principals have complied with the escrow instructions.

THE GENERAL PROVISIONS PRINTED ABOVE HAVE BEEN READ AND ARE HEREBY APPROVED BY THE UNDERSIGNED.

These escrow instructions, and amendments hereto, may be executed in one or more counterparts, each of which independently shall have the same effect as if it were the original, and all of which taken together shall constitute one and the same instruction.

(Optional)

Name___BILL BUYER_____ Tax Payers I.D. # _____

(Optional)

Name___BETTY BUYER_____ Tax Payers I.D. # _____

Address_____ Phone_____

SELLER

I approve of the foregoing instructions and agree to sell and will deliver to you papers, instruments and/or funds required from me (within the "time limit date" specified herein), which you are authorized to deliver when you can issue your policy of title insurance as set forth above. I agree to pay any personal property taxes properly chargeable to me. You are instructed to use the money and record the instruments, to comply with said instructions and to pay all encumbrances of record necessary without further approval including prepayment penalties to show title as herein provided. I agree to pay your usual sellers escrow fee, drawing of documents and such other charges which are advanced for my account regardless of the consummation of this escrow. I also agree to pay the policy of title insurance premium and recording fees which are properly chargeable to me and documentary transfer tax in the amount of $ AS REQU. which you are instructed to enter on the deed and affix your signature thereto, if required. In the event this amount is incorrect, you are authorized and instructed to enter the correct amount on the deed and deduct the additional cost therefore from funds accruing to my account. In the event an incorrect amount is entered on the deed and said deed is recorded, I hereby hold you harmless and agree to reimburse you for any loss you may sustain by said amount being incorrect.

At the close of this transaction you are authorized to pay commission in the amount of $ 12,000.00 _____

to: $6,000.00 to Decade 40 Real Estate and
      $6,000.00 to Warm Springs-Teller Real Estate

Broker's License No.

(Optional)

Name_____ Tax Payers I.D. # _____
       I. M. STADIN, Executor of the
Name Estate of N.O. Longerhere, deceased Tax Payers I.D. # _____

(Optional)

Address_____ Phone_____

First American Title Insurance Company

_____Santa Ana_____ CALIFORNIA • TELEPHONE _(714) 558-3211_

ESCROW INSTRUCTIONS

BUYER

ESCROW SUMMARY	
PAID OUTSIDE ESCROW	$
CASH THROUGH ESCROW	200,000.00
ENCUMBRANCE OF RECORD	
ENCUMBRANCE OF RECORD	
PURCHASE MONEY ENCUMB.	
TOTAL CONSIDERATION	$200,000.00

Escrow Officer_____

Ref. Number _12345-RF_____

Date   October 16, 1989

To FIRST AMERICAN TITLE_____

I hereby agree to purchase the hereinafter described property for a total consideration of $ 200,000.00   and will
on or before   November 30, 1989   hand you said consideration which is payable as follows:

$20,000.00 has been paid outside of escrow and Seller acknowledges receipt of
same, the balance of $180,000.00 is to be deposited into escrow prior to close
of escrow.

I will deliver to you any additional funds and execute any instruments which are necessary to comply with the terms hereof, all of
which you may use when you hold for me an Executors Deed executed by

I. M. STANDIN, Executor of the Estate of N. O. Longerhere, deceased

Form 9-B, Page 1
Escrow Instructions: IAEA

and when you can issue your
liability of $ 200,000.00
County of   Comfort

Owners

coverage form policy of title insurance with
on the following described property situated in the City of   Heavenly
, State of California:

Lot 101 in Block 5, as Designated on the map entitled "Heavenly Ranchos,
Heavenly, California", which map was filed in the office of the Recorder of
the County of Comfort, State of California, on February 29, 1942, in volume 26
of maps, at page 916.

Property commonly known as   10 Best Place, Heavenly, California   90000

showing title vested in: BILL BUYER and BETTY BUYER, husband and wife as joint tenants.

free of encumbrances except:
1.   Current
General and special taxes for fiscal year 19 89 - 19 90
2. The lien of supplemental taxes which may be assessed as a result of revised assessed values.
3. Assessments and/or Bonds
4. Covenants, conditions, restrictions, rights of way, easements, and reservations, as described in that certain preliminary title
    evidence, issued, or to be issued, herein.
5.

Buyer understatnds that the seller is authorized to sell the property pursuant to
the Independent Administration of Estates Act contained in the California Probate
Code ("the IAEA"). The closing of this escrow is subject to and conditioned upon
either notice of sale being given pursuant to the provisions set forth in Section
10580 of said Code, and no objection or revocation of consent being received; or
all required consents being received pursuant to Section 10582 of said Code.

It is understood between the parties hereto that subject property is being
purchased in its "AS IS" condition.

1039-1
(Rev. 2-86)

Form 9-B, Page 2
Escrow Instructions: IAEA

ESCROW INSTRUCTIONS — Page 2

If instructed by the parties prorate and/or adjust the following as of   close of escrow

x☒ 1. Taxes based on the amount of the last tax statement of the Tax Collector issued prior to the close of escrow. (If the amount of the new tax bill issued by the Tax Collector after close of escrow is more or less than the amount used for proration purposes, the difference, if any, will be adjusted by the parties herein outside of escrow.) Sellers are to forward to buyers any present or future tax bills on property herein.

☐ 2. Insurance (including FHA mortgage insurance, if any).

☐ 3. Interest on all existing trust deeds, improvements assessments and/or bonds taken over by buyers.

☐ 4. Rental per rent statement handed you.

☐ 5. Charge the buyer and credit the seller the amount of any funds held in an impound account, if any, in connection with an existing loan.

☐ 6. You are to hold for me   shares of water stock of the   Company.

☐ 7.

I hereby agree to pay any charges including usual buyers escrow fee and any advances and expenses that are properly chargeable to me regardless of the consummation of this escrow. At the close of escrow you are to mail all documents, checks, etc., to the person entitled thereto at the address shown in these instructions.

GENERAL PROVISIONS

1.   **Deposit of Funds & Disbursements**

You shall deposit all funds received in this escrow in any bank insured by an agency of the United States Government, including your affiliated bank, First American Trust Company, in one or more of your general escrow demand accounts. These funds may be transferred to any other general escrow demand account or accounts, in the above named bank or banks, including those maintained in your affiliated bank. All disbursements shall be made by your check. You are authorized not to close escrow or disburse until good funds have been confirmed in escrow.

2.   **Prorations and Adjustments**

The expression "close of escrow" used in this escrow means the date of which instruments referred to herein are recorded and relates only to prorations and/or adjustments unless otherwise specified.

All prorations and/or adjustments are to be made on the basis of a 30-day month unless otherwise instructed in writing.

3.   **Recordation of Instruments**

You are authorized to record any documents delivered through this escrow, the recording of which is necessary or proper in the issuance of the requested policy of title insurance.

Form 9-B, Page 3
Escrow Instructions: IAEA

4. **Authorization to Execute Assignment of Insurance Policies**

You are to execute on behalf of the parties hereto form assignments of interest in any insurance policies (other than title insurance) called for in this escrow; forward assignments and policies upon close of escrow to the agent with the request, first, that insurer consent to such transfer and/or attach a loss-payable clause and/or make such other additions or corrections as may have been specifically required herein, and second, that the agent thereafter forward such policies to the parties entitled to them.

In all acts in this escrow relating to insurance, including adjustments, if any, you shall be fully protected in assuming that each policy is in force and that the necessary premium therefor has been paid.

5. **Authorization to Furnish Copies**

You are to furnish a copy of these instructions, amendments thereto, closing statements and/or any other documents deposited in this escrow to the lender or lenders, the real estate broker or brokers and/or the attorney or attorneys involved in this transaction upon request of the lenders, brokers or attorneys.

6. **Personal Property Taxes**

No examination or insurance as to the amount or payment of personal property taxes is required unless specifically requested.

7. **Right of Cancellation**

Any party instructing you to cancel this escrow shall file notice of cancellation in your office, in writing. You shall within a reasonable time thereafter mail, by certified mail, one copy of the notice to each of the other parties at the addresses stated in this escrow. Unless written objection to cancellation is filed in your office by a party within ten (10) days after date of mailing, you are authorized at your option to comply with the notice an demand payment of your cancellation charges as provided in this agreement. If written objection is filed, you are authorized at your option to hold all money and instruments in this escrow and take no further action until otherwise directed, either by the parties' mutual written instructions, or final order of a court of competent jurisdiction.

8. **Action in Interpleader**

The parties hereto expressly agree that you, as escrow holder, have the absolute right at your election to file an action in interpleader requiring the parties to answer and litigate their several claims and rights among themselves and you are authorized to deposit with the clerk of the court all documents and funds held in this escrow. In the event such action is filed, the parties jointly and severally agree to pay your cancellation charges and costs, expenses and reasonable attorney's fees which you are required to expend or incur in the interpleader action, the amount thereof to be fixed and judgment therefor to be rendered by the court. Upon the filing of the action, you shall thereupon be fully released and discharged from all obligations to further perform any duties or obligations otherwise imposed by the terms of this escrow.

9. **Termination of Agency Obligations**

If there is no action taken on this escrow within six (6) months after the "time limit date" as set forth in the escrow instructions or written extension thereof, your agency obligation shall terminate at your option and all documents, monies or other items held by you shall be returned to the parties depositing same.

In the event of cancellation of this escrow, whether it be at the request of any of the parties or otherwise, the fees and charges due First American Title Insurance Company, including expenditures incurred and/or authorized shall be borne equally by the parties hereto (unless otherwise agreed to specifically).

5080-2
Rev 2-80

Form 9-B, Page 4
Escrow Instructions: IAEA

ESCROW INSTRUCTIONS — Page 3

10. Conflicting Instructions

Should you before or after close of escrow receive or become aware of any conflicting demands or claims with respect to this escrow or the rights of any of the parties hereto, or any money or property deposited herein or affected hereby, you shall have the right to discontinue any or all further acts on your part until the conflict is resolved to your satisfaction, and you shall have the further right to commence or defend any action or proceedings for the determination of the conflict as provided in paragraphs 7 and 8 of these General Provisions.

11. Funds Retained in Escrow

If for any reason funds are retained in escrow, you may deduct therefrom _____ $10.00 _____ as a monthly charge as custodian thereof.

12. Usury

You are not to be concerned with any question of usury in any loan or encumbrances involved in the processing of this escrow and you are hereby released of any responsibility or liability therefor.

13. Indemnify for Attorneys Fees and Costs

In the event suit is brought by any party to this escrow, including the title company or any other party, as against each other, or others, including the title company, claiming any right they may have as against each other or against the title company, then in that event, the parties hereto agree to indemnify and hold harmless the title company against any attorney's fees and costs incurred by it.

14. Amendments to Escrow Instructions

Any Amendment or supplement to these escrow instructions must be in writing. These escrow instructions constitute the entire escrow between the escrow holder and the parties hereto.

15. Foreign Investment in Real Property Tax Act

The Foreign Investment in Real Property Tax Act of 1980 as amended by the Tax Reform Act of 1984 places special requirements for tax reporting and withholding on the parties to a real estate transaction where the transferor (seller) is a non-resident alien or non-domestic corporation or partnership or is a domestic corporation or partnership controlled by non-residents or non-resident corporations or partnerships. The parties to this transaction are seeking an attorney's, accountant's or other tax specialist's opinions concerning the effect of this Act on this transaction and are not acting on any statements made or omitted by the escrow or closing officer.

_____   _____
Buyer   Seller

Form 9-B, Page 5
Escrow Instructions: IAEA

TIME IS OF THE ESSENCE OF THESE INSTRUCTIONS. If this escrow is not in condition to close by   January 15   19 90 , and demand for cancellation is received by you from any party to this escrow after said date, you shall act in accordance with the cancellation instructions contained in the general provisions on the previous page hereof. If no demand for cancellation is made, you will proceed to close this escrow when the principals have complied with the escrow instructions.

THE GENERAL PROVISIONS PRINTED ABOVE HAVE BEEN READ AND ARE HEREBY APPROVED BY THE UNDERSIGNED.

These escrow instructions, and amendments hereto, may be executed in one or more counterparts, each of which independently shall have the same effect as if it were the original, and all of which taken together shall constitute one and the same instruction.

(Optional)

Name_____ Tax Payers I.D. # _____

    Bill Buyer

(Optional)

Name_____ Tax Payers I.D. # _____

    Betty Buyer

Address_____ Phone_____

SELLER

I approve of the foregoing instructions and agree to sell and will deliver to you papers, instruments and/or funds required from me (within the "time limit date" specified herein), which you are authorized to deliver when you can issue your policy of title insurance as set forth above. I agree to pay any personal property taxes properly chargeable to me. You are instructed to use the money and record the instruments, to comply with said instructions and to pay all encumbrances of record necessary without further approval including prepayment penalties to show title as herein provided. I agree to pay your usual sellers escrow fee, drawing of documents and such other charges which are advanced for my account regardless of the consummation of this escrow. I also agree to pay the policy of title insurance premium and recording fees which are properly chargeable to me and documentary transfer tax in the amount of $ as requ. which you are instructed to enter on the deed and affix your signature thereto, if required. In the event this amount is incorrect, you are authorized and instructed to enter the correct amount on the deed and deduct the additional cost therefore from funds accruing to my account. In the event an incorrect amount is entered on the deed and said deed is recorded, I hereby hold you harmless and agree to reimburse you for any loss you may sustain by said amount being incorrect.

At the close of this transaction you are authorized to pay commission in the amount of $12,000.00 _____
to: $6,000.00 to Decade 40 Real Estate and
    $6,000.00 to Warm Springs-Teller Real Estate

                                                  Broker's License No.

(Optional)

Name_____ Tax Payers I.D. # _____
    I. M. Standin, Executor of the

(Optional)

Name Estate of N. O Longerhere, deceased Tax Payers I.D. # _____

Address_____ Phone_____

NOTES

COMMISSION CHECK

Chapter 7

Closing the Escrow

 The escrow company will need two documents which the attorney should provide:

Order Confirming Sale of Real Property.

The escrow company has to have a certified copy of the order. Allow two weeks for the attorney to prepare the order, file it with the court and send a certified copy to the escrow. (See Form 10 at the end of this chapter.)

Executor's or Administrator's Deed.

Either the attorney for the representative or the escrow company will prepare this deed.

The deed must be signed by the representative before a notary public. (See Form 11 at the end of this chapter.)

Since the deed is one of the last documents required to close the sale, inquire of the escrow company and the attorney as to who will prepare the deed. If the attorney prepares the deed, you may want to follow up to make sure the deed is signed by the representative and delivered to the escrow company.

As soon as the escrow company has the necessary documentation from the attorney and representative, i.e., the order confirming sale and the deed, you can direct your attention to making sure that the remainder of the requirements to close escrow have been fulfilled, such as loan documents, etc.

By this time, with the close of escrow at hand, you will probably not be required to contact the attorney again. Your practical understanding of a probate sale will not go unnoticed by either the attorney or the representative. They both will be appreciative of your prompt attention to the details, enabling the sale to close with minimum hassle. Your rewards: the self-satisfaction of a job well done and, of course, the commission check when the escrow closes.

The Game Can Get Complicated

Title to the couple's house was held in community property. Both spouses died and left different beneficiaries.

The wife specified in her Will that her community property would go to their children. The husband said in his Will that his one-half community property was to go to charities. Each representative of the two estates was represented by an attorney.

Four dominoes in this play:

- *Domino 1: wife's estate — seller of one-half interest*

- *Domino 2: husband's estate — seller of one-half interest*

- *Domino 3: buyer of both one-half interests*

- *Domino 4: overbidder in court.*

The main asset in each estate was the one-half interest in the residence. Each side was attempting to draw parallel sale documents, because the two representatives of the estates could not agree to the terms.

It was difficult to find a buyer who would be involved in a multi-domino play. The right hand did not know what the left hand was doing.

The complexity of the transaction for the selling agent was to coordinate the buyer, the representatives, the agents, the court date and to get papers drawn in a compatible manner.

The agent for the seller was getting conflicting information from each attorney. Each attorney was interpreting the laws differently as far as the estate's obligation to pay certain customary transfer taxes. The probate court normally prefers an "as is" sale, but there are exceptions to the rule. In this sale the purchase agreement called for a substantial amount of repairs for the structural pest control work and for a defunct furnace. The buyer's loan approval took the repair work into consideration. One attorney wanted to take repairs off the gross purchase price.

The problem:

Attorney #1 said one-half estate interest worth $150,000 and drew papers for that price.

Attorney #2 said one-half estate interest worth $150,000 less the cost of repairs.

$$
\begin{array}{rr}
 & \$150,000 \\
\text{repairs cost} & \underline{(12,500)} \\
 & 138,500
\end{array}
$$

He drew papers based on a sales price of $138,500.

The lender would only loan on the property based on the gross price. The lender did not want to accept the second method of figuring the gross price. Then the lender did not want to accept the loan at all. These problems caused considerable delays.

After all the delays, an overbidder was successful at the hearing.

The agent stated, however, that even though the sale was time-consuming she would always accept a probate sale listing.

A probate sale presents great unknowns, which, if undertaken by you with the proper attitude, will present a challenge, broaden your real estate career and make the next probate sale experience easier.

ATTORNEY OR PARTY WITHOUT ATTORNEY *(Name and Address)*:	TELEPHONE NO.:
☐ RECORDING requested by and return to:	(415) 100-1000
JOHN Q. LAWYER	
100 City Justice Building	FOR COURT USE ONLY
Heavenly, CA 90000	

ATTORNEY FOR *(Name)*: Petitioner

SUPERIOR COURT OF CALIFORNIA, COUNTY OF COMFORT

STREET ADDRESS: Court Building
MAILING ADDRESS: Court Building
CITY AND ZIP CODE: Heavenly, CA 900000
BRANCH NAME:

ESTATE OF (NAME): N. O. LONGERHERE

[X] DECEDENT ☐ CONSERVATEE ☐ MINOR

ORDER CONFIRMING SALE OF REAL PROPERTY ☐ And Confirming Sale of Other Property as a Unit	CASE NUMBER: 10000

1. Hearing date: 11/15/89   Time: 9:00 a.m.   Dept.: 3   Rm.:

FOR RECORDER'S USE

THE COURT FINDS

2. All notices required by law were given and, if required, proof of notice of sale was made.
3. a. [X] Sale was authorized or directed by the will
   b. ☐ Good reason existed for the sale
   of the property commonly described as *(street address or location)*:
   10 Best Place
   Heavenly, CA 90000
4. The sale was legally made and fairly conducted.
5. The confirmed sale price is not disproportionate to the value of the property.
6. [X] Private sale: The amount bid is 90% or more of the appraised value of the property as appraised within one year of the date of the hearing.
7. An offer exceeding the amount bid by the statutory percentages
   [X] cannot be obtained ☐ was obtained in open court. The offer complies with all applicable law.
8. The personal representative has made reasonable efforts to obtain the highest and best price reasonably attainable for the property

THE COURT ORDERS

9. The sale of the real property legally described [X] on reverse ☐ in Attachment 9
   ☐ and other property sold as a unit described ☐ on reverse ☐ in Attachment 9a
   is confirmed to *(name)*: BILL and BETTY BUYER

   (manner of vesting title): joint tenants

   for the sale price of: $ 200,000   on the following terms *(use attachment or reverse if necessary)*:
   See reverse

10. The personal representative *(name)*: I. M. STANDIN
    is directed to execute and deliver a conveyance of the estate's interest in the property described in item 9
    ☐ and other property described in item 9 upon receipt of the consideration for the sale.

11. a. [X] No additional bond is required.
    b. ☐ Personal representative shall give an additional bond for: $, surety, or otherwise, as provided by law.
    c. ☐ Net sale proceeds shall be deposited by escrow holder in a blocked account to be withdrawn only on court order. Receipts shall be filed. *(Specify institution and location)*:

12. a. ☐ No commission is payable.
    b. [X] A commission from the proceeds of the sale is approved in the amount of: $ 12,000
       to be paid as follows: $6,000 to Decade 40 Real Estate
       $6,000 to Warm Springs-Teller Real Estate

Date:

▶

JUDGE OF THE SUPERIOR COURT

☐ Signature follows last attachment

13. ☐ Number of pages attached: 14. ☐ Legal description on reverse.

Form Approved by the
Judicial Council of California
DE-265, GC-065 (Rev. July 1, 1988)

ORDER CONFIRMING SALE OF REAL PROPERTY
(Probate)

Probate Code, §§ 2543, 10313

Form 10, Page 1
Order Confirming Sale of Real Property

ESTATE OF (NAME): N. O. LONGERHERE	CASE NUMBER: 10000

15. [X] **Legal description** of the [X] real property ☐ personal property in item 9 *(describe)*:

Lot 101 in Block 5, as Designated on the map entitled "Heavenly Ranchos, Heavenly, California", which map was filed in the office of the Recorder of the County of Comfort, State of California, on February 29, 1942, in Volume 26 of maps, at page 916.

TERMS OF SALE:

Property is sold in an "AS IS" condition.
Purchase price $200,000
Cash down   20,000
Balance cash $180,000 payable before close of escrow.

Taxes to be prorated as of close of escrow.
Seller to pay for examination of title, policy of title insurance, recording of conveyance and tranfer taxes.

Escrow charges to be paid 1/2 by seller and 1/2 by buyer.

(SEAL)	**CLERK'S CERTIFICATE**
	I certify that the foregoing Order Confirming Sale of Real Property, including any attached description of real or personal property, is a true and correct copy of the original on file in my office.
	Date: _____ CLERK, by _____ , Deputy

Form 10, Page 2
Order Confirming Sale of Real Property

RECORDED AT THE REQUEST OF
AND WHEN RECORDED MAIL TO:

MAIL TAX STATEMENTS TO:

APN#: 559-54-3227

EXECUTOR'S DEED

I. M. STANDIN, as Executor of the Estate of N. O. LONGERHERE, Deceased, in consideration of the sum of TWO HUNDRED THOUSAND DOLLARS ($200,000.00) cash, receipt of which is hereby acknowledged, do hereby grant and convey to BILL BUYER and BETTY BUYER, husband and wife, as joint tenants, all right, title and interest of N. O. LONGERHERE, Deceased, and all right, title and interest that the Estate of N. O. LONGERHERE, Deceased, may have acquired by operation of law, or otherwise, in and to improved real property located in the City of Heavenly, County of Comfort, State of California, commonly known as 10 Best Place, Heavenly, California, and legally described as follows:

Lot 101 of Block 5, as Designated on the map entitled "Heavenly Ranchos, Heavenly, California," which map was filed in the office of the Recorder of the County of Comfort, State of California, on February 29, 1942, in Volume 26 of maps, at page 916.

Form 11, Page 1
Executor's/Administrator's Deed

This deed is made pursuant to the Order Confirming Sale of Real Property made in the matter of the Estate of N. O. LONGERHERE, Deceased, in the Heavenly County Superior Court of the State of California, Case No. 10000, filed on December 15, 1989, a certified copy of which Order is recorded contemporaneously herewith in the Office of the County Recorder of Comfort County, reference to which is hereby made.

IN WITNESS WHEREOF, this instrument is executed on the 16th day of December, 1989, at Heavenly, California.

_____
I. M. STANDIN, as
Executor of the Estate of
N. O. LONGERHERE, Deceased

STATE OF CALIFORNIA   )
COUNTY OF COMFORT   )

On this 16th day of December, 1989, before me, the undersigned, a Notary Public in and for said County and State, personally appeared I. M. STANDIN, personally known to me, or proven to me on the basis of satisfactory evidence, to be the person whose name is subscribed to the foregoing instrument, and he acknowledged to me that he executed the same.

WITNESS my hand and official seal.

_____
Notary Public in and for said
County and State

**Form 11, Page 2
Executor's/Administrator's Deed**

NOTES

Chapter 8

Mobile Homes, Cooperatives and Timeshare Units

These are some special situations which you will encounter from time to time and it will be helpful to know how to handle them.

Condominiums

Condominiums are interests in real property and are sold as such, unless the interest is held as a limited partnership.

Community or Cooperative Apartments, Timeshare Units

Community or cooperative apartments are personal property (stock) with a right to occupancy and may be sold as personal property. Timeshare units, although considered personal property, are sold according to the same provisions relating to real property.

Overbids are computed on the same basis as sales in real property. Broker's commission is allowed according to the same guidelines as in real property sales. (See Chapter 5.)

The prospective buyer should obtain acceptance of a Board of Directors of a community or cooperative apartment before petitioning the court for confirmation of sale.

Mobile Homes and Mobile Home Parks

If a Mobile Home Is for Sale.

Mobile home ownership can be confusing. Formerly, mobile homes were classified as vehicles and registered by the state Department of Motor Vehicles (DMV). Effective July 1, 1981, the responsibility for registering mobile homes was transferred to the state Department of Housing and Community Development (HCD).

Small travel trailers, and some older mobile homes, will still have DMV pink slips. A mobile home is defined by the state as :

A structure, designed and equipped for human habitation, transportable in one or more sections, which requires a permit in order to be moved on the highway. The condition of requiring a permit for being towed on the highway means that the unit is greater than 40 feet in overall length or over eight and one-half feet in overall width.

Some mobile homes built before 1981 meeting this definition are still registered with the DMV, and should be transferred from the DMV to Housing and Community Development records.

Therefore, the first thing you should do is ask to see the registration and determine whether the mobile home is registered under the DMV or the HCD. This will determine which agency you are dealing with, but the rules for transfer of ownership are the same for both.

Almost all mobile homes large enough to require the services of a realtor for a sale will come under the regulations of the Department of Housing and Community Development. This department publishes a booklet titled *Guide to Basic Mobilehome Transfers*, intended to be used by escrow agents, dealers, and realtors, and I would advise you to request a copy, as it covers more than probate transfers.

When you are involved in the sale of a mobile home in the case of a death, look at the registration and see how title was held, as the requirements for transfer differ.

Single Owner: If the estate is in probate, the executor or administrator can sell the mobile home.

When Both the Mobile Home and the Land Are Being Sold: When both the mobile home and the land are being sold, follow the same procedures as in the sale of real property with personal property included. (See Chapters 3, 4, 5, 6 and 7.)

The mobile home and the land can be sold under the Independent Administration of Estates Act (IAEA). (See Chapter 2.)

When the Mobile Home Is Being Sold by Itself: A mobile home can be sold under the Independent Administration of Estates Act (IAEA.) (See Chapter 2.)

Before you list the property, read Chapter 3, "Prior to Signing the Listing Agreement." The same procedures apply.

When you are ready to list the property, read Chapter 4, "The Listing Agreement." The same procedures also apply except that the listing agreement for mobile homes is different. A form of listing agreement when the mobile home has been registered for at least one year under Part 2 of Division 13 of the California Health and Safety Code is included at the end of this chapter. The wording to add when the sale is a probate sale is contained in paragraph 16 of the sample listing agreement (Form 12, Exclusive Authorization and Right to Sell — Mobile Home).

Read Chapter 5, "Accepting an Offer," for the procedures when you have a buyer. The sale contract for a mobile home is different from the one used in real property. A form of the Mobile Home Purchase Contract and Receipt for Deposit when the mobile home has been registered at least one year under Part 2 of Division 13 of the California Health and Safety Code is contained at the end of this chapter

(Form 13). The wording to add in a probate sale is set forth in paragraph 21 on page 4 of the sample form.

If the sale is to go through an escrow, read Chapter 6, "Opening the Escrow," and Chapter 7, "Closing the Escrow." The transfer of title must be accompanied by a certified copy of the Letters Testamentary or Letters of Administration, showing the personal representative's appointment. Ask the attorney for the personal representative to supply you with a certified copy. The administrator or executor signs for the deceased registered owner on line 1 of the DMV pink slip or the HCD certificate of title as: _____[name]_____, executor/administrator of the Estate of __[name of decedent].

Transfer Without Probate by Certificate: When the owner of the mobile home dies leaving no other property requiring probate and 40 days have elapsed since the date of death, the mobile home can be transferred with a Certificate for Transfer Without Probate. Inquire if there is an attorney advising regarding the decedent's affairs. The attorney will more than likely prepare the certificate.

The certificate can be signed by either an heir (a relative) who has a right to succeed to the property of the decedent, or by a beneficiary who has a right to the property under the Will, even though the Will is not being probated. The person has to certify that:

- The decedent left no property necessitating probate and no probate proceeding is now being or has been conducted.

- The mobile home has not been bequeathed to anyone else.
- He or she is an heir under the Probate Code or a beneficiary under the Will.
- No one has a right to the decedent's unit that is superior to his or her right.
- There are no unsecured creditors whose claims remain unsatisfied.

The heir or beneficiary can sign for the deceased registered owner on the DMV pink slip or HCD certificate of title as: [name of decedent] by ___[name]___, heir/beneficiary.

Joint ownership, names joined by "or": title to the unit passes to the surviving co-owner(s). The surviving owner can sign on line 1 of the title to release all owner interests. No substantiating documentation is needed, unless another co-owner term is also on the title, such as JTRS or COMPRO.

Joint ownership, names joined by "and": the interest of the deceased co-owner may only be released by the heir of the deceased on a Certificate for Transfer Without Probate, or, if the estate was probated, by the executor or administrator with a certified copy of the Letters. Title passes to the surviving co-owner or, with the surviving co-owner's release, to a new owner.

Joint tenants with the right of survivorship, "JTRS": the interest of the deceased party passes to the surviving co-owner. A copy of the deceased owner's death certificate substitutes for the missing signature.

Tenants in common: now things become even more complicated.

Names joined by "TENCOM": for title certificates issued prior to January 1, 1985, with title reading this way, one owner's signature releases ownership. No substitute is needed for the deceased owner's signature.

Names joined by "TENCOM OR": the interest of the deceased party may be released with a signature of a surviving co-owner, with no other documents needed.

Names joined by "TENCOM AND": the interest of the decedent passes to the decedent's heir and may be released by the heir with a Certificate for Transfer Without Probate or by an executor or administrator with a certified copy of Letters.

Community property, "COMPRO": upon the death of either the husband or the wife, the interest of the deceased spouse passes to his or her heir and may be released by the heir with a Certificate for Transfer Without Probate or by an administrator or executor with a certified copy of Letters.

Sales Procedures. A mobile home in most instances is subject to an agreement. The mobile owner may pay rent to allow the mobile to be situated on the land. In some instances the mobile home owner may own the land on which the mobile sits and an undivided interest in the common areas, like a condominium or townhouse. There is more than likely a rental agreement or the association bylaws which set out the park rules. In either instance, the Civil

Code sets out in detail the requirements to advertise a mobile home for sale, exchange or rent.

If not prohibited by the terms of an agreement with the management or association, a sign may be displayed:

- In the window of the mobile home; and/or

- On the side of the mobile home facing the street. The sign can state the name, address and telephone number of the person to contact and must not exceed 24 inches wide by 18 inches high.

In some instances the park management or association may show or list the mobile. In that event, the owner's written authorization setting out the terms and conditions must first be obtained (Civil Code Sections 798.70 and 798.71).

Also, the management or association cannot charge a fee for assisting in the sale unless a service is performed. The service which the seller requests must be in writing.

The management or association cannot require that the mobile home be removed from the park after it is sold, unless:

- The mobile home is less than 10 feet wide; or

- The mobile home is more than 20 years old, or more than 25 years old if manufactured after September 15, 1971, and is 20 feet wide or more and does not comply with Sections 18550,

18552 and 18605 of the Health and Safety Code; or

- The mobile home is more than 17 years old, or more than 25 years old if manufactured after September 15, 1971, and is less than 20 feet wide and does not comply with the construction and safety standards under Sections 18550, 18552 and 18605 of the Health and Safety Code; or

- The mobile home is in a seriously run-down condition and does not meet the health and safety codes.

The burden is on the management to prove that the mobile is in a seriously run-down condition or in disrepair (Civil Code Section 798.73).

Check to see if the rental or association agreement requires that the management approve the prospective purchaser or if the management must be given written notice of the sale prior to close of the sale. If the prospective buyer has the financial ability to pay the rent and charges of the park, the management cannot refuse to approve the prospective buyer. The exception to the foregoing statement is that if the management can prove the conduct of the prospective purchaser at prior parks was such that he or she would not comply with the rules and regulations of the park, approval can be withheld (Civil Code Section 798.74[a]).

The management is allowed to charge the prospective purchaser a fee to obtain a financial report or credit rating, the fee to then be a credit toward the first month's rent. If the prospective purchaser is rejected by the management, then the management must refund the fee within 30 days from date of rejection. If the prospective purchaser elects not to purchase the mobile, management has the option of keeping the fee to help defray administration costs (Civil Code Section 798.74[b]).

The escrow or sale agreement must contain a statement, signed by the prospective purchaser, that the purchaser agrees to the terms of the rental or association agreement. Providing the escrow company with the rental agreement, signed by the purchaser and management, will fulfill this requirement (Civil Code Section 798.75).

If the owner of a mobile home dies and ownership of the mobile passes to an heir or joint tenant, that person has the right to sell the mobile home to a third person. However, all of the owner's responsibilities to the management regarding rent, utilities and reasonable maintenance of the mobile and its premises have to be met up until the date the mobile home is resold.

If the Mobile Home Park Is for Sale.

If you are listing a mobile home park for sale and the park has a resident organization, the owner may have to provide written notice to the resident organization. The notice must be given not less than 10 days but no more than 30 days prior to signing the listing agreement for the sale of the park, or making an offer to sell the park to anyone.

However, notice only has to be given if the resident organization has notified the park owner or manager in writing that the park residents are interested in purchasing the park, and has provided the names and addresses of the officers to whom notice should be made.

If the proper notice has not been given, it does not affect the validity of the sale or the ability of a real estate broker to collect a commission, but the seller could be subject to a lawsuit by the park residents or resident organization.

This is another instance where you should contact the attorney before proceeding with the listing agreement. So, first call the attorney for the seller to see if the notice procedure, if necessary, has been completed before you ask the seller to sign the listing agreement (Civil Code Section 798.80).

140 Inside a Probate Sale

EXCLUSIVE AUTHORIZATION AND RIGHT TO SELL

(MOBILE HOME registered at least one year under Part 2 of Division 13 of Health and Safety Code)

THIS IS INTENDED TO BE A LEGALLY BINDING AGREEMENT. READ IT CAREFULLY.

CALIFORNIA ASSOCIATION OF REALTORS® (CAR) STANDARD FORM

1. EXCLUSIVE RIGHT TO SELL: I hereby employ and grant _____ 19____,
hereafter called "Broker", the exclusive and irrevocable right commencing on _____ 19____,
and expiring at midnight on _____
to sell or exchange the mobile home located at _____
_____ City of _____,
_____, California in _____, Mobile Home Park,
County of _____
Space #_____ described as follows: Manufacturer's name/ID _____ Model_____ Year (DOM)_____ This unit was measured ☐ Yes ☐ No
Year (DFS)_____ Width_____ Net Length_____ Expando_____ Type_____
Trade Name _____ Bedrooms_____ Baths_____ Exterior_____ Roof_____ Skirting_____
Serial #'s _____ Label/Insignia   19____ License/Decal # _____ LPT Tax Roll/In Lieu Tax Exp. Date

	U				
	X	(A)			/
	XX	(B)			/
	XXX	(C)			/

together with all built in appliances, heating units, water heater and the following equipment:
Refrigerator _____ Range_____ Oven_____ Washer_____ Dryer_____
Disposer_____ Dishwasher_____ Air Conditioner Serial # _____ Brand_____ Type_____
Carport Awning _____ Patio Awning_____ Porch_____ Screen Rm._____ Shed _____
Wheels_____ Tires_____ Other _____

Park Information

Type _____ Clubhouse_____ Swimming Pool_____ Gas_____ Electricity_____
Guests_____ Pets_____ Cable TV_____ Space Rental $ _____ /mo. Deposit_____
Rent includes: ☐ Space, ☐ Water, ☐ Sewer, ☐ Garbage-Trash, ☐ Common Area Maintenance, ☐ Natural Gas
☐ Electricity, ☐ other _____
Name of Manager _____ Phone No._____
Senior Adult Park ☐ Yes ☐ No   Family Park ☐ Yes ☐ No   Park Approval Required ☐ Yes ☐ No
Has Seller obtained written agreement from Park Management permitting over age mobile home to remain (Civil Code § 798.73)? ☐ Yes ☐ No

2. TERMS OF SALE: The purchase price shall be _____
Dollars ($_____), to be paid as follows: _____
_____
_____
_____
_____
_____

Form 12, Page 1
Exclusive Authorization and Right to Sell — Mobile Home

The following additional items of personal property are to be included in the above-stated price:

_____

_____

_____

_____

_____

_____

3. MULTIPLE LISTING SERVICE (MLS): Broker is a Participant of_____
ASSOCIATION/BOARD OF REALTORS® Multiple Listing Service (MLS) and this listing information will be provided to the MLS to be published and disseminated to its Participants in accordance with its Rules and Regulations.
Broker is authorized to cooperate with other real estate brokers, to appoint subagents and to report the sale, its price, terms and financing for the publication, dissemination, information and use by authorized Association/Board members, MLS Participants and Subscribers.

4. TITLE AND COMPLIANCE WITH MOBILE HOME LAWS:

(a) I hereby agree to deliver the above described mobile home and personal property, if any, free of liens and encumbrances, recorded, filed, registered, or known to me.

(b) Evidence of title shall be in form of a duly endorsed, dated and delivered Certificate of Ownership of mobile home and delivery of current Registration Certificate of Title as required by law.

(c) I warrant that the above described mobile home complies with the equipment requirements of the Health and Safety Code and the regulations of the Department of Housing and Community Development, HUD regulations, and any applicable local ordinance and is either 1) located within an established mobile home park as defined in California Health and Safety Code § 18214 and that advertising or offering it for sale is not contrary to any provision of any contract between me and the mobile park ownership, or 2) located pursuant to a local zoning ordinance or permit, on a lot where its presence has been authorized or its continued presence and such use would be authorized for a total and uninterrupted period of at least one year.

(d) I agree to deliver as soon as possible to Broker for submission to Buyer a copy of my lease or rental agreement and all current park rules and regulations and inform Broker of any changes occurring during the term hereof.

Seller acknowledges receipt of a copy of this page, which constitutes Page 1 of_____ Pages.

Seller's Initials (_____) (_____)

OFFICE USE ONLY
Reviewed by Broker or Designee_____
Date _____

EXCLUSIVE AUTHORIZATION AND RIGHT TO SELL (MHL-14 PAGE 1 OF 2)

Form 12, Page 2
Exclusive Authorization and Right to Sell — Mobile Home

Subject Mobile Home Address _____

Notice: The amount or rate of real estate commissions is not fixed by law. They are set by each Broker individually and may be negotiable between the Seller and Broker.

COMPENSATION TO BROKER: I hereby agree to compensate Broker, irrespective of agency relationships(s), as follows:

5. (a) _____ percent of the selling price, or $_____ if the mobile home is sold during the term hereof, or any extension thereof, by Broker on the terms herein set forth or any other price and terms I may accept, or through any other person, or by me, or _____ percent of the price shown in 2, or $_____ , if said mobile home is withdrawn from sale, transferred, conveyed, leased, rented without the consent of Broker, or made unmarketable by my voluntary act during the term hereof or any extension thereof.

   (b) the compensation provided for in subparagraph (a) above if the mobile home is sold, conveyed or otherwise transferred within _____ calendar days after the termination of this authority or any extension thereof to anyone with whom Broker has had negotiations prior to final termination, provided I have received notice in writing, including the names of the prospective purchasers, before or upon termination of this agreement or any extension hereof. However, I shall not be obligated to pay the compensation provided for in subparagraph (a) if a valid listing agreement is entered into during the term of said protection period with another licensed real estate broker and a sale, lease or exchange of the mobile home is made during the term of said valid listing agreement.

   (c) I authorize Broker to cooperate with other brokers, to appoint subagents, and to divide with other brokers such compensation in any manner acceptable to brokers.

   (d) In the event of an exchange, permission is hereby given Broker to represent all parties and collect compensation or commissions from them, provided there is full disclosure to all principals of such agency. Broker is authorized to divide with other brokers such compensation or commissions in any manner acceptable to brokers.

   (e) If requested by Broker, Seller shall execute and deliver an escrow instruction irrevocably assigning Broker's compensation in an amount equal to the compensation provided in subparagraph (a) (above) from the Seller's proceeds.

6. **DEPOSIT:** Broker is authorized to accept and hold on Sellers behalf a deposit on the account of the purchase price.

7. **HOME PROTECTION PLAN:** Seller is informed that home protection plans are available. Such plans may provide additional protection and benefit to a Seller and Buyer. Cost and coverage may vary.

*8. **KEYBOX:** I authorize Broker to install a KEYBOX.   (initial) YES (____/____) NO (____/____)

9. **SIGN:** Authorization to install a FOR SALE/SOLD sign on the mobile home in accordance   (initial) YES (____/____) NO (____/____) with applicable law and park rules.

10. **PEST CONTROL:** Seller shall furnish a current Structural Pest Control Report.   (initial) YES (____/____) NO (____/____)

*11. **TAX WITHHOLDING:** Seller agrees to perform any act reasonably necessary to carry out the provisions of FIRPTA (Internal Revenue Code § 1445) and California Revenue and Taxation Code §§ 18805 and 26131, and regulations promulgated thereunder.

12. **DISCLOSURE:** I agree to hold Agent harmless from any liability arising from any incorrect information supplied by me, or from any material fact known by me concerning the mobile home, the park or other location in which it is located, which I fail to disclose.

13. **EQUAL HOUSING OPPORTUNITY:** This mobile home is offered in compliance with federal, state, and local anti-discrimination laws.

*14. **ARBITRATION OF DISPUTES:** Any dispute or claim in law or equity arising out of this contract or any resulting transaction shall be decided by neutral binding arbitration in accordance with the rules of the American Arbitration Association, and not by court action except as provided by California law for judicial review of arbitration proceedings. Judgment upon the award rendered by the arbitrator(s) may be entered in any court having jurisdiction thereof. The parties shall have the right to discovery in accordance with Code of Civil Procedure § 1283.05. The following matters are excluded from arbitration hereunder: (a) a judicial or non-judicial foreclosure or other action or proceeding to enforce a deed of trust, mortgage, or real property sales contract as defined in Civil Code § 2985, (b) an unlawful detainer action, (c) the filing or enforcement of a mechanic's lien, (d) any matter which is within the jurisdiction of a probate court, or (e) an action for bodily injury or wrongful death, or for latent or patent defects to which Code of Civil Procedure § 337.1 or § 337.15 applies. The filing of a judicial action to enable the recording of a notice of pending action, for order of attachment, receivership, injunction, or other provisional remedies, shall not constitute a waiver of the right to arbitrate under this provision.

Form 12, Page 3
Exclusive Authorization and Right to Sell — Mobile Home

"NOTICE: BY INITIALLING IN THE SPACE BELOW YOU ARE AGREEING TO HAVE ANY DISPUTE ARISING OUT OF THE MATTERS INCLUDED IN THE 'ARBITRATION OF DISPUTES' PROVISION DECIDED BY NEUTRAL ARBITRATION AS PROVIDED BY CALIFORNIA LAW AND YOU ARE GIVING UP ANY RIGHTS YOU MIGHT POSSESS TO HAVE THE DISPUTE LITIGATED IN A COURT OR JURY TRIAL. BY INITIALLING IN THE SPACE BELOW YOU ARE GIVING UP YOUR JUDICIAL RIGHTS TO DISCOVERY AND APPEAL, UNLESS THOSE RIGHTS ARE SPECIFICALLY INCLUDED IN THE 'ARBITRATION OF DISPUTES' PROVISION. IF YOU REFUSE TO SUBMIT TO ARBITRATION AFTER AGREEING TO THIS PROVISION, YOU MAY BE COMPELLED TO ARBITRATE UNDER THE AUTHORITY OF THE CALIFORNIA CODE OF CIVIL PROCEDURE. YOUR AGREEMENT TO THIS ARBITRATION PROVISION IS VOLUNTARY."

"WE HAVE READ AND UNDERSTAND THE FOREGOING AND AGREE TO SUBMIT DISPUTES ARISING OUT OF THE MATTERS INCLUDED IN THE 'ARBITRATION OF DISPUTES' PROVISION TO NEUTRAL ARBITRATION."

(Initial) BROKER (_____) SELLER (_____ / _____)

15. **ATTORNEY'S FEES:** In any action, proceeding or arbitration arising out of this agreement, the prevailing party shall be entitled to reasonable attorney's fees and costs.
16. **ADDITIONAL TERMS:** Sale subject to consent of all heirs/beneficiaries or confirmation of court.
17. **ENTIRE AGREEMENT:** I, the Seller, warrant that I am the owner of the mobile home or have the authority to execute this agreement. The Seller and Broker further intend that this agreement constitutes the complete and exclusive statement of its terms and that no extrinsic evidence whatsoever may be introduced in any judicial or arbitration proceeding, if any, involving this agreement.
    I acknowledge that I have read and understand this agreement, including the information on the reverse side, and have received a copy.
18. **CAPTIONS:** The captions in this agreement are for convenience of reference only and are not intended as part of this agreement.

Date _____ , 19_____   _____ , California

Seller _____   Address _____

Seller _____   City_____ State_____ Phone_____

In consideration of the above, Broker agrees to use diligence in procuring a purchaser.

Real Estate Broker _____   By_____

Address _____   City_____ State_____ Phone_____

*REFER TO REVERSE SIDE FOR ADDITIONAL INFORMATION

Copyright© 1989. CALIFORNIA ASSOCIATION OF REALTORS®
525 South Virgil Avenue, Los Angeles, California 90020

OFFICE USE ONLY
Reviewed by Broker or Designee _____
Date _____

EQUAL HOUSING
OPPORTUNITY

EXCLUSIVE AUTHORIZATION AND RIGHT TO SELL (MHL-14 PAGE 2 OF 2)

MOBILE HOME PURCHASE CONTRACT AND RECEIPT FOR DEPOSIT
(MOBILE HOME registered at least one year under Part 2 of Division 13 of Health and Safety Code)
THIS IS MORE THAN A RECEIPT FOR MONEY. IT IS INTENDED TO BE A LEGALLY BINDING CONTRACT. READ IT CAREFULLY.
CALIFORNIA ASSOCIATION OF REALTORS® (CAR) STANDARD FORM

_____ , California _____ , 19 _____

Received from _____ Dollars $ _____
herein called Buyer, the sum of _____
evidenced by ☐ cash, ☐ cashier's check, ☐ personal check, or ☐ _____ , payable to _____
_____ , to be held uncashed until acceptance of this offer, as deposit on account of purchase price of
_____ Dollars $ _____

for the purchase of mobile home located at _____ , City of _____
County of _____ , California in _____ Mobile Home Park,
Space # _____ described as follows: Manufacturer's name/ID _____ Model _____ Year (DOM) _____
Year (DFS) _____ Width _____ Net Length _____ Expando _____ Type _____ This unit was measured ☐ Yes ☐ No
Trade Name _____ Bedrooms _____ Baths _____ Exterior _____ Roof _____ Skirting _____

Serial #'s		Label/Insignia	19 __ License/Decal #	LPT Tax Roll/In Lieu Tax Exp. Date
_____	U	_____	_____	_____ / _____
_____	X (A)	_____	_____	_____ / _____
_____	XX (B)	_____	_____	_____ / _____
_____	XXX (C)	_____	_____	_____ / _____

together with all built in appliances, heating units, water heater and the following equipment:
Refrigerator _____ Range _____ Oven _____ Washer _____ Dryer _____
Disposer _____ Dishwasher _____ Air Conditioner Serial # _____ Brand _____ Type _____
Carport Awning _____ Patio Awning _____ Porch _____ Screen Rm. _____ Shed _____
Wheels _____ Tires _____ Other _____
☐ and for the purchase of real property, situated in _____ , County of _____
described as follows: _____ .

1. **FINANCING:** The obtaining of Buyer's financing is a contingency of this agreement.
   A. DEPOSIT upon acceptance, to be deposited into _____ $ _____
   B. INCREASED DEPOSIT within _____ days of Seller's acceptance to be deposited into _____ $ _____
   C. BALANCE OF DOWN PAYMENT to be deposited into _____ on or before _____ $ _____
   D. Buyer to apply, qualify for and obtain a NEW FIRST LOAN in the amount of .... $ _____
   secured by a Security Agreement and Certificate of Title designating lender as legal owner, payable monthly at
   approximately $ _____ including interest at origination not to exceed _____ %, per annum, ☐ fixed rate,
   ☐ other _____
   all due _____ years from date of origination. Loan fee not to exceed _____ .
   Seller agrees to pay a maximum of _____ VA/FHA discount points. Additional terms _____
   _____

   E. Buyer ☐ to assume, ☐ to take title subject to an EXISTING FIRST LOAN with an approximate balance of .... $ _____
   In favor of _____ payable monthly at $ _____ including interest at _____ % ☐ fixed rate,
   ☐ other _____ Fees not to exceed _____ .
   Disposition of impound account _____ .
   Additional terms _____

Form 13, Page 1
Mobile Home Purchase Contract and Receipt for Deposit

F. Buyer to execute a Note in the amount of $_____ IN FAVOR OF SELLER, secured by a Security Agreement designating Seller as lienholder and perfected as a ☐ first, ☐ second, ☐ third, ☐_____ lien or HCD approved Statement of Lien, or other appropriate HCD approved document(s), payable monthly at $_____ ☐ or more, including interest at_____ %, all due_____ years from date of origination ☐ or upon sale or transfer of subject mobile home or any real property which is included in the sale. A late charge of_____ shall be due on any installment not paid within_____ days of the due date. Additional terms _____
_____

G. In the event Buyer assumes or takes title subject to an existing loan, Seller shall provide Buyer with copies of applicable notes and Security Agreements. A loan may contain a number of features which affect the loan, such as interest rate changes, monthly payment changes, balloon payments, etc. Buyer shall be allowed_____ calendar days after receipt of such copies to notify Seller in writing of disapproval. FAILURE TO NOTIFY SELLER IN WRITING SHALL CONCLUSIVELY BE CONSIDERED APPROVAL. Buyer's approval shall not be unreasonably withheld. Difference in existing loan balances shall be adjusted in ☐ Cash, ☐ Other _____ .

H. Buyer agrees to act diligently and in good faith to obtain all applicable financing.

I. ADDITIONAL FINANCING TERMS:_____
_____
_____
_____
_____

J. TOTAL PURCHASE PRICE . . . . $_____

2. PARK RULES: Buyer acknowledges that Seller is not assigning or subletting the space the mobile home occupies in its present location. Within _____ calendar days of acceptance of the offer, Buyer shall deliver to Seller's agent a completed Park Application together with Buyer's approval of the Park Rules and Regulations. Buyer's application is subject to Mobile Park Management approval. Failure of approval shall terminate this agreement and Buyer's deposit shall be returned.

3. UPGRADES. ☐ Buyer ☐ Seller shall be responsible for upgrades required by mobile park management.

4. SUPPLEMENTS: The ATTACHED supplements are incorporated herein:
    ☐ HCD Certificate of Retail Value and Purchase Price   ☐ _____
    ☐ VA and FHA Amendments (CAR FORM VA/FHA-11)   ☐ _____

Buyer and Seller acknowledge receipt of a copy of this page, which constitutes Page 1 of_____ Pages.
Buyer's Initials (_____) (_____) Seller's Initials (_____) (_____)

OFFICE USE ONLY
Reviewed by Broker or Designee _____
Date

MOBILE HOME PURCHASE CONTRACT AND RECEIPT FOR DEPOSIT (MHD-14 PAGE 1 OF 4)

SI Mar 89

Form 13, Page 2
Mobile Home Purchase Contract and Receipt for Deposit

Subject Mobile Home Address _____

5. **ESCROW:** Buyer and Seller shall deliver signed instructions to _____ the escrow holder, within _____ calendar days from Seller's acceptance which shall provide for closing within _____ calendar days from Seller's acceptance. Escrow fees to be paid as follows: _____
_____ .

6a. **TITLE (MOBILE HOME):** Title to the mobile home is to be free of liens and encumbrances, recorded, filed, registered, or known to Seller, except as set forth above. Evidence of title shall be by delivery of (a) a duly endorsed and dated Certificate of Ownership and (b) a current Registration Certificate, as required by law. If Seller is unable to deliver title as herein provided, Buyer may terminate this agreement and the deposit shall be returned to Buyer.

6b. **TITLE (REAL PROPERTY):** Title to any real property which is included in the sale is to be free of liens, encumbrances, easements, restrictions, rights, and conditions of record or known to Seller, other than the following: (a) current property taxes, (b) covenants, conditions, restrictions, and public utility easements of record, if any, provided the same do not adversely affect the continued use of the property for the purposes for which it is presently being used, unless reasonably disapproved by Buyer in writing within_____ calendar days of receipt of current preliminary report furnished at_____ expense, and (c) _____ . Seller shall furnish Buyer at_____ expense a California Land Title Association policy issued by_____ Company, showing title vested in Buyer subject only to the above. If Seller is unwilling or unable, or fails, to eliminate any title matter disapproved by Buyer as above, or to deliver title as above, Buyer may terminate this agreement and the deposit shall be returned to Buyer.

7. **VESTING:** Unless otherwise designated in the escrow instructions of Buyer, title shall vest as follows: _____
_____ .
(The manner of taking title may have significant legal and tax consequences. Therefore, give this matter serious consideration.)

8a. **PRORATIONS (MOBILE HOME):** Property taxes, interest, rents, association dues, premiums on insurance acceptable to Buyer, Park rent, license fee assumed by Buyer, and _____ shall be paid current and prorated as of: ☐ Close of Escrow, or ☐ _____ . IF THE MOBILE HOME IS ON PROPERTY TAX ROLL, IT WILL BE REASSESSED UPON CHANGE OF OWNERSHIP. THIS WILL AFFECT THE TAXES TO BE PAID. A supplemental tax bill will be issued, which shall be paid as follows: (a) for periods after close of escrow, by Buyer (or by final acquiring party if part of an exchange), and (b) for periods prior to close of escrow, by Seller. TAX BILLS ISSUED AFTER CLOSE OF ESCROW SHALL BE HANDLED DIRECTLY BETWEEN BUYER AND SELLER.

8b. **PRORATIONS (REAL PROPERTY):** Property taxes, payments on bonds and assessments assumed by Buyer, interest, rents, association dues, premiums on insurance acceptable to Buyer, and _____ shall be paid current and prorated as of: ☐ the day of recordation of the deed; or ☐ _____ . Bonds or assessments now a lien shall be ☐ paid current by Seller, payments not yet due to be assumed by Buyer; or ☐ paid in full by Seller, including payments not yet due; or ☐ _____ . County Transfer tax shall be paid by_____ . The_____ transfer tax or transfer fee shall be paid by_____ PROPERTY WILL BE REASSESSED UPON CHANGE OF OWNERSHIP. THIS WILL AFFECT THE TAXES TO BE PAID. A supplemental tax bill will be issued, which shall be paid as follows: (a) for periods after close of escrow, by Buyer (or by final acquiring party if part of an exchange), and (b) for periods prior to close of escrow, by Seller. TAX BILLS ISSUED AFTER CLOSE OF ESCROW SHALL BE HANDLED DIRECTLY BETWEEN BUYER AND SELLER.

9. **POSSESSION:** Possession and occupancy shall be delivered to Buyer, ☐ on close of escrow, or ☐ not later than_____ days after close of escrow, or ☐ _____ .

10. **KEYS:** Seller shall, when possession is available to Buyer, provide keys and/or means to operate all locks, and alarms, if any.

Form 13, Page 3
Mobile Home Purchase Contract and Receipt for Deposit

11. **FIXTURES:** All permanently installed fixtures and fittings that are attached to the mobile home or for which special openings have been made are included in the purchase price, including electrical, light, plumbing and heating fixtures, built-in appliances, screens, awnings, shutters, all window coverings, attached floor coverings, T.V. antennas, air cooler or conditioner, mailbox, if any, and _____ _____ except _____ .

12. **SMOKE DETECTOR(S):** State law requires that mobile homes be equipped with an operable smoke detector. Local law may have additional requirements. If required by state and/or local law, Seller shall deliver to Buyer a written statement of compliance prior to close of escrow.

13. **MOVING:** Buyer acknowledges that present or future movement of the mobile home is limited by law and is subject to the regulations of the Department of Transportation.

14. **DESTRUCTION:** If the mobile home is materially damaged or destroyed prior to close of escrow, then, on demand of Buyer, any deposit made by Buyer shall be returned to Buyer and this agreement terminated.

15. **TAX WITHHOLDING:** Under the Foreign Investment in Real Property Tax Act (FIRPTA), IRC § 1445, *every* Buyer of U.S. real property *must*, unless an exemption applies, deduct and withhold from Seller's proceeds 10% of the gross sales price. Under California Revenue and Taxation Code § § 18805 and 26131, the Buyer must deduct and withhold an additional one-third of the amount required to be withheld under federal law. The primary FIRPTA exemptions are: No withholding is required if (a) Seller provides Buyer with an affidavit under penalty of perjury, that Seller is not a "foreign person," or (b) Seller provides Buyer with a "qualifying statement" issued by the Internal Revenue Service, or (c) Buyer purchases real property for use as a residence and the purchase price is $300,000 or less and Buyer or a member of Buyer's family has definite plans to reside at the property for at least 50% of the number of days it is in use during each of the first two twelve-month periods after transfer. Seller and Buyer agree to execute and deliver as directed any instrument, affidavit, or statement reasonably necessary to carry out those statutes and regulations promulgated thereunder.

16. **MULTIPLE LISTING SERVICE:** If Broker is a Participant of an Association/Board multiple listing service ("MLS"), the Broker is authorized to report the sale, its price, terms, and financing for the publication, dissemination, information, and use of the authorized Board members, MLS Participants and Subscribers.

17. **ADDITIONAL TERMS AND CONDITIONS:**
ONLY THE FOLLOWING PARAGRAPHS A THROUGH I *WHEN INITIALLED BY BOTH BUYER AND SELLER* ARE INCORPORATED IN THIS AGREEMENT.

Buyer's Initials   Seller's Initials

_____ / _____   _____ / _____   **A. PHYSICAL AND GEOLOGICAL INSPECTION:** Buyer shall have the right, at Buyer's expense, to select a licensed contractor and/or other qualified professional(s), to make "Inspections" (including tests, surveys, or other studies, inspections, and investigations) of the subject property, including but not limited to structural, plumbing, sewer/septic system, well, heating, electrical, built-in appliances, roof, soils, foundation, mechanical systems, pool, pool heater, pool filter, air conditioner, if any, possible environmental hazards such as asbestos, formaldehyde, radon gas and other substances/products, and geologic conditions. Buyer shall keep the subject property free and clear of any liens, indemnify and hold Seller harmless from all liability, claims, demands, damages, or costs, and repair all damages to the property arising from the Inspections.

All claimed defects concerning the condition of the property that adversely affect the continued use of the property for the purposes for which it is presently being used (☐ or as _____) shall be in writing, supported by written reports, if any, and delivered to Seller within _____ calendar days FOR "INSPECTIONS" OTHER THAN GEOLOGICAL, and/or within _____ calendar days FOR GEOLOGICAL "INSPECTIONS," **of acceptance of the offer.** Buyer shall furnish Seller copies, at no cost, of all reports concerning the property obtained by Buyer. When such reports disclose conditions or information unsatisfactory to the Buyer, which the Seller is unwilling or unable to correct, Buyer may cancel this agreement. Seller shall make the premises available for all inspections. BUYER'S FAILURE TO NOTIFY SELLER IN WRITING SHALL CONCLUSIVELY BE CONSIDERED APPROVAL.

Buyer and Seller acknowledge receipt of copy of this page, which constitutes Page 2 of _____ Pages.

Buyer's Initials (_____) (_____)   Seller's Initials (_____) (_____)

```
┌─────── OFFICE USE ONLY ───────┐
│ Reviewed by Broker or Designee ____ │
│          Date ____            │
└───────────────────────────────┘
```

MOBILE HOME PURCHASE CONTRACT AND RECEIPT FOR DEPOSIT (MHD-14 PAGE 2 OF 4)

SF Mar 89

Form 13, Page 4
Mobile Home Purchase Contract and Receipt for Deposit

Subject Mobile Home Address _____

Buyer's Initials   Seller's Initials

_____/_____   _____/_____   **B. CONDITION OF PROPERTY:** Seller warrants, through the date possession is made available to Buyer:
(1) the mobile home and the improvements on the property on which it is located, including landscaping, grounds and pool/spa, if any, shall be maintained in the same condition as upon the date of acceptance of the offer, and (2) the roof is free of all known leaks, and (3) built-in appliances, and water, sewer/septic, plumbing, heating, electrical, air conditioning, pool/spa systems, if any, are operative, and (4) Seller shall replace all broken and/or cracked glass; (5) _____

Buyer's Initials   Seller's Initials

_____/_____   _____/_____   **C. SELLER REPRESENTATION:** Seller warrants that Seller has no knowledge of any notice of violations of City, County, State, Federal, Building, Zoning, Fire, HCD Compliance, Health Codes or ordinances, or other governmental regulation filed or issued against the mobile home and property. This warranty shall be effective until date of close of escrow.

Buyer's Initials   Seller's Initials

_____/_____   _____/_____   **D. PEST CONTROL: (1)** Within _____ calendar days of acceptance of the offer, Seller shall furnish Buyer at the expense of ☐ Buyer, ☐ Seller, a current written report of an inspection by _____ , a licensed Structural Pest Control Operator, of the main building, ☐ detached garage(s) or carport(s), if any, and ☐ the following other structures on the property: _____
(2) If requested by either Buyer or Seller, the report shall separately identify each recommendation for corrective measures as follows:
    "Section 1": Infestation or infection which is evident.
    "Section 2": Conditions that are present which are deemed likely to lead to infestation or infection.
(3) If no infestation or infection by wood destroying pests or organisms is found, the report shall include a written Certification as provided in Business and Professions Code § 8519(a) that on the date of inspection "no evidence of active infestation or infection was found."
(4) All work recommended to correct conditions described in "Section 1," shall be at the expense of ☐ Buyer, ☐ Seller.
(5) All work recommended to correct conditions described in "Section 2," if requested by Buyer, shall be at the expense of ☐ Buyer, ☐ Seller.
(6) The repairs shall be performed with good workmanship and materials of comparable quality and shall include repairs of leaking showers, replacement of tiles and other materials removed for repairs. It is understood that exact restoration of appearance or cosmetic items following all such repairs is not included.
(7) Funds for work agreed to be performed after close of escrow, shall be held in escrow and disbursed upon receipt of a written Certification as provided in Business and Professions Code § 8519(b) that the inspected property "is now free of evidence of active infestation or infection".
(8) Work to be performed at Seller's expense may be performed by Seller or through others, provided that (a) all required permits and final inspections are obtained, and (b) upon completion of repairs a written Certification is issued by a licensed Structural Pest Control Operator showing that the inspected property "is now free of evidence of active infestation or infection."
(9) If inspection of inaccessible areas is recommended by the report, Buyer has the option to accept and approve the report, or within _____ calendar days from receipt of the report to request in writing further inspection be made. BUYER'S FAILURE TO NOTIFY SELLER IN WRITING OF SUCH REQUEST SHALL CONCLUSIVELY BE CONSIDERED APPROVAL OF THE REPORT. If further inspection recommends "Section 1" and/or "Section 2" corrective measures, such work shall be at the expense of the party designated in subparagraph (4) and/or (5), respectively. If no infestation or infection is found, the cost of inspection, entry and closing of the inaccessible areas shall be at the expense of Buyer.
(10) Other _____

Buyer's Initials   Seller's Initials

_____/_____   _____/_____   **E. FLOOD HAZARD AREA DISCLOSURE:** Buyer is informed that subject property is situated in a "Special Flood Hazard Area" as set forth on a Federal Emergency Management Agency (FEMA) "Flood Insurance Rate Map" (FIRM) or "Flood Hazard Boundry Map" (FHBM). The law provides that, as a condition of obtaining financing on most structures located in a "Special Flood Hazard Area," lenders require flood insurance where the property or its attachments are security for a loan.
    The extent of coverage and the cost may vary. For further information consult the lender or insurance carrier. No representation or recommendation is made by the Seller and the Broker(s) in the transaction as to the legal effect or economic consequences of the National Flood Insurance Program and related legislation.

Form 13, Page 5
Mobile Home Purchase Contract and Receipt for Deposit

Buyer's Initials   Seller's Initials

_____ / _____   _____ / _____   **F. SPECIAL STUDIES ZONE DISCLOSURE:** Buyer is informed that subject property is situated in a Special Studies Zone as designated under § § 2621-2625, inclusive, of the California Public Resources Code; and, as such, the construction or development on this property of any structure for human occupancy may be subject to the findings of a geologic report prepared by a geologist registered in the State of California, unless such a report is waived by the City or County under the terms of the act.

Buyer is allowed _____ calendar days from acceptance of the offer to make further inquiries at appropriate governmental agencies concerning the use of the subject property under the terms of the Special Studies Zone Act and local building, zoning, fire, health, and safety codes. When such inquiries disclose conditions or information unsatisfactory to the Buyer, which the Seller is unwilling or unable to correct, Buyer may cancel this agreement. BUYER'S FAILURE TO NOTIFY SELLER IN WRITING SHALL CONCLUSIVELY BE CONSIDERED APPROVAL.

Buyer's Initials   Seller's Initials

_____ / _____   _____ / _____   **G. HOME PROTECTION PLAN:** Buyer and Seller have been informed that Home Protection Plans are available. Such plans may provide additional protection and benefit to a Seller or Buyer. California Association of Realtors® and the Broker(s) in this transaction do not endorse or approve any particular company or program:

a) ☐ A Buyer's coverage Home Protection Plan to be issued by _____

Company, at a cost not to exceed $ _____ , to be paid by ☐ Seller, ☐ Buyer; or

b) ☐ Buyer and Seller elect not to purchase a Home Protection Plan.

Buyer's Initials   Seller's Initials

_____ / _____   _____ / _____   **H. LIQUIDATED DAMAGES: If Buyer fails to complete said purchase by reason of any default of Buyer, Seller shall be released from the obligation to sell the mobile home to Buyer and may proceed against Buyer upon any claim or remedy which Seller may have in law or equity; provided, however, that by initialling this paragraph Buyer and Seller agree that Seller shall retain the deposit as Seller's liquidated damages, and that it would be impractical and extremely difficult to fix actual damages suffered because of such default; that the amount paid by Buyer as deposit constitutes a reasonable estimate and agreed stipulation of such damages. Buyer and Seller agree to execute a similar liquidated damages provision for any increased deposits. (Funds deposited in trust accounts or in escrow are not released automatically in the event of a dispute. Release of funds requires written agreement of the parties, judicial decision or arbitration.)**

Buyer and Seller acknowledge receipt of copy of this page, which constitutes Page 3 of _____ Pages.

Buyer's Initials (_____) (_____)   Seller's Initials (_____) (_____)

```
┌─── OFFICE USE ONLY ───┐
│ Reviewed by Broker or Designee _____ │
│                                        │
│ Date _____                           │
└────────────────────────────────────────┘
```

EQUAL HOUSING OPPORTUNITY

SF-Mar-89

MOBILE HOME PURCHASE CONTRACT AND RECEIPT FOR DEPOSIT (MHD-14 PAGE 3 OF 4)

Form 13, Page 6
Mobile Home Purchase Contract and Receipt for Deposit

Subject Mobile Home Address _____

I. ARBITRATION OF DISPUTES: Any dispute or claim in law or equity arising out of this contract or any resulting transaction shall be decided by neutral binding arbitration in accordance with the rules of the American Arbitration Association, and not by court action except as provided by California law for judicial review of arbitration proceedings. Judgment upon the award rendered by the arbitrator(s) may be entered in any court having jurisdiction thereof. The parties shall have the right to discovery in accordance with Code of Civil Procedure § 1283.05. The following matters are excluded from arbitration hereunder: (a) a judicial or non-judicial foreclosure or other action or proceeding to enforce a deed of trust, mortgage, or real property sales contract as defined in Civil Code § 2985, (b) an unlawful detainer action, (c) the filing or enforcement of a mechanic's lien, (d) any matter which is within the jurisdiction of a probate court, or (e) an action for bodily injury or wrongful death, or for latent or patent defects to which Code of Civil Procedure § 337.1 or § 337.15 applies. The filing of a judicial action to enable the recording of a notice of pending action, for order of attachment, receivership, injunction, or other provisional remedies, shall not constitute a waiver of the right to arbitrate under this provision. Any dispute or claim by or against broker(s) and/or associate licensee(s) participating in this transaction shall be submitted to arbitration consistent with the provision above only if the broker(s) and/or associate licensee(s) making the claim or against whom the claim is made shall have agreed to submit it to arbitration consistent with this provision.
"NOTICE: BY INITIALLING IN THE SPACE BELOW YOU ARE AGREEING TO HAVE ANY DISPUTE ARISING OUT OF THE MATTERS INCLUDED IN THE 'ARBITRATION OF DISPUTES' PROVISION DECIDED BY NEUTRAL ARBITRATION AS PROVIDED BY CALIFORNIA LAW AND YOU ARE GIVING UP ANY RIGHTS YOU MIGHT POSSESS TO HAVE THE DISPUTE LITIGATED IN A COURT OR JURY TRIAL. BY INITIALLING IN THE SPACE BELOW YOU ARE GIVING UP YOUR JUDICIAL RIGHTS TO DISCOVERY AND APPEAL, UNLESS THOSE RIGHTS ARE SPECIFICALLY INCLUDED IN THE 'ARBITRATION OF DISPUTES' PROVISION. IF YOU REFUSE TO SUBMIT ARBITRATION AFTER AGREEING TO THIS PROVISION, YOU MAY BE COMPELLED TO ARBITRATE UNDER THE AUTHORITY OF THE CALIFORNIA CODE OF CIVIL PROCEDURE. YOUR AGREEMENT TO THIS ARBITRATION PROVISION IS VOLUNTARY."
"WE HAVE READ AND UNDERSTAND THE FOREGOING AND AGREE TO SUBMIT DISPUTES ARISING OUT OF THE MATTERS INCLUDED IN THE 'ARBITRATION OF DISPUTES' PROVISION TO NEUTRAL ARBITRATION."

Buyer's Initials   Seller's Initials

_____/_____   _____/_____

18. **ATTORNEY'S FEES:** In any action, proceeding or arbitration arising out of this agreement, the prevailing party shall be entitled to reasonable attorney's fees and costs.

19. **ENTIRE CONTRACT:** Time is of the essence. All prior agreements between the parties are incorporated in this agreement which constitutes the entire contract. Its terms are intended by the parties as a final expression of their agreement with respect to such terms as are included herein and may not be contradicted by evidence of any prior agreement or contemporaneous oral agreement. The parties further intend that this agreement constitutes the complete and exclusive statement of its terms and that no extrinsic evidence whatsoever may be introduced in any judicial or arbitration proceeding, if any, involving this agreement.

20. **CAPTIONS:** The captions in this agreement are for convenience of reference only and are not intended as part of this agreement.

21. **OTHER TERMS AND CONDITIONS:** Sale is subject to consent of all heirs/beneficiaries
or confirmation of court. _____
_____
_____
_____
_____

22. **AGENCY CONFIRMATION:** The following agency relationship(s) are hereby confirmed for this transaction:
LISTING AGENT: _____ is the agent of (check one):
(PRINT FIRM NAME)

☐ the Seller exclusively; or ☐ both the Buyer and Seller

SELLING AGENT: _____ (If not the same as Listing Agent) is the agent of (check one):
(PRINT FIRM NAME)

☐ the Buyer exclusively; or ☐ the Seller exclusively; or ☐ both the Buyer and Seller.

23. **AMENDMENTS:** This agreement may not be amended, modified, altered or changed in any respect whatsoever except by a further agreement in writing executed by Buyer and Seller.

Form 13, Page 7
Mobile Home Purchase Contract and Receipt for Deposit

24. **OFFER:** This constitutes an offer to purchase the described property. Unless acceptance is signed by Seller and the signed copy delivered in person, by mail, or facsimile, and received by Buyer at the address below, or by _____ who is authorized to receive it, on behalf of Buyer, within _____ calendar days of the date hereof, this offer shall be deemed revoked and the deposit shall be returned. Buyer has read and acknowledges receipt of a copy of this offer. This agreement and any supplement, addendum or modification relating hereto, including any photocopy or facsimile thereof, may be executed in two or more counterparts, all of which shall constitute one and the same writing.

REAL ESTATE BROKER _____   BUYER_____

By _____   BUYER_____
Address _____   Address _____

_____
Telephone _____   Telephone _____

ACCEPTANCE

The undersigned Seller accepts and agrees to sell the property on the above terms and conditions and agrees to the above confirmation of agency relationships (☐ subject to attached counter offer).

Seller agrees to pay to Broker(s) _____
compensation for services as follows: _____

Payable: (a) On recordation of the deed or other evidence of title, or (b) if completion of sale is prevented by default of Seller, upon Seller's default, or (c) if completion of sale is prevented by default of Buyer, only if and when Seller collects damages from Buyer, by suit or otherwise, and then in an amount not less than one-half of the damages recovered, but not to exceed the above fee, after first deducting title and escrow expenses and the expenses of collection, if any. Seller shall execute and deliver an escrow instruction irrevocably assigning the compensation for service in an amount equal to the compensation agreed to above. In any action, proceeding, or arbitration between Broker(s) and Seller arising out of this agreement, the prevailing party shall be entitled to reasonable attorneys fees and costs. The undersigned has read and acknowledges receipt of a copy of this agreement and authorizes Broker(s) to deliver a signed copy to Buyer.

Date _____ Telephone_____   SELLER _____
Address _____

_____   SELLER _____

Real Estate Broker(s) agree to the foregoing.

Broker_____ By _____ Date_____

Broker_____ By _____ Date_____

This form is available for use by the entire real estate industry. The use of this form is not intended to identify the user as a REALTOR. REALTOR is a registered collective membership mark which may be used only by real estate licensees who are members of the NATIONAL ASSOCIATION OF REALTORS and who subscribe to its Code of Ethics.

Page 4 of_____ Pages.

OFFICE USE ONLY
Reviewed by Broker or Designee _____
Date _____

EQUAL HOUSING OPPORTUNITY
SF Mar-89

MOBILE HOME PURCHASE CONTRACT AND RECEIPT FOR DEPOSIT (MHD-14 PAGE 4 OF 4)

Form 13, Page 8
Mobile Home Purchase Contract and Receipt for Deposit

NOTES

Chapter 9

Community Property

 When the title to property is held as community property and passes outright to the surviving spouse, in most instances, no probate is required. The summary proceeding, outside of probate, is called a Spousal Property Petition.

Spousal Set Aside Procedure

In this procedure, community property and other property passes to the surviving spouse. It is used:

- When a husband or wife dies intestate (without a Will) and leaves property

"Each spouse owns one-half of the community property."

that passes to the surviving spouse without probate administration; or

- When the husband or wife dies testate (with a Will) and in his or her Will gives the property to the surviving spouse (Probate Code Section 13500).

Under California law, upon the death of a married person, one-half of the community property belongs to the surviving spouse and the other one-half belongs to the deceased spouse (Probate Code Section 100). When the decedent's one-half "community" interest is passing to the surviving spouse, in most instances, no probate is required.

There are exceptions, however, such as tax considerations or creditor situations, when the attorney for the surviving spouse may decide to probate the entire community property estate. Another exception would be if the deceased spouse willed his or her one-half community property interest to another person other than the surviving spouse. In that event a probate might be necessary. (See example at end of Chapter 7.)

In addition, this set-aside procedure may be used for any property which the deceased spouse in his or her Will leaves to the surviving spouse. In other words, the separate property of the decedent may be passed to the surviving spouse by using this spousal property procedure.

We will deal in this section with the deceased spouse's property passing to the surviving spouse. The procedures to transfer the title of the deceased spouse are simplified but still require the probate court's order. This procedure is called a "spousal set aside" petition.

The surviving spouse cannot sell the community (or quasi-community property, obtained while living in another state) until after 40 days from the spouse's death (Probate Code Section 13540). After the 40 days have elapsed, he or she can sell the property without probate or during probate administration, unless someone else has recorded an order claiming an interest in the property under the Will of the deceased spouse.

After Your First Contact with the Client.

When contacted by a surviving spouse who is ready to sell the property, first ask the surviving spouse or the attorney the date of death. Knowing the date of death will determine your lead time to do your homework. Remember, you cannot list the property until 40 days have lapsed.

Call the surviving spouse's attorney (who may not necessarily be the attorney for the estate). Tell the attorney you have been contacted by the surviving spouse to handle the sale of the property. In a spousal set aside procedure, no personal representative is appointed by the court. Therefore, the surviving spouse can sign the listing agreeent.

Listing the Property.

Your listing the property and the attorney preparing the spousal property petition can be handled simultaneously. As you know, according to California real estate law, one-half of the property technically belongs to the surviving spouse but title must be transferred into her name before she can legally sell it.

Spousal Property Petition.

While you are listing and showing the property, the attorney will prepare the spousal property petition. The petition will basically request the court:

- To make a determination that the deceased spouse's one-half interest passes to the surviving spouse without probate administration (Probate Code Section 13500).

- To confirm that one-half of the community property belongs to the surviving spouse (Probate Code Section 100 and 101).

Appraisal of Assets.

The appraisal procedure is different than in a probate proceeding. The inventory contains a list of the community property assets and need not be appraised for the court to approve the spousal property petition.

However, an appraisal is usually obtained to establish a tax basis. So, the petition will almost always ask for a probate referee to be appointed. The attorney will send the community property inventory to the referee for appraisal. However, the appraised inventory does not need to be filed with the court prior to the hearing date on the spousal property petition.

Hearing on the Petition.

The hearing on the spousal property petition will be set in three to four weeks from the time it is filed. If the paperwork is in order, no appearances are necessary and the court will probably recommend the matter for approval. Ask the attorney to let you know the hearing date and then call the attorney the day before the hearing to make sure the matter will be approved. Ask the attorney when the escrow can expect to receive a certified copy of the spousal property order. (See Form 14 at the end of this chapter.)

Closing the Escrow.

If you are in a hurry to close the escrow, volunteer to attend the hearing and "walk" the order through. Then you can personally deliver the order to the escrow. Otherwise, ask the attorney to send the escrow a certified copy of the community property order.

When the escrow receives the spousal property order, if all other paperwork in the escrow is in order, the escrow can close and you will receive your commission check. The surviving spouse will appreciate your prompt and knowledgeable attention and service. Just think about the referrals you will receive!

Attorney or Party without Attorney *(Name and Address):*

JOHN Q. LAWYER
100 City Justice Building
Suite 200
Heavenly, CA 90000

Telephone No.: (415) 100-1000

For Court Use Only

Attorney for *(Name):* Petitioner

SUPERIOR COURT OF CALIFORNIA, COUNTY OF COMFORT
STREET ADDRESS: Court Building
MAILING ADDRESS: Court Building
CITY AND ZIP CODE: Heavenly, CA 900000
BRANCH NAME:

ESTATE OF (NAME): N. O. LONGERHERE

Decedent

SPOUSAL PROPERTY ORDER	Case Number: 10000

1. Date of hearing: 11/15/89   Time: 9:00 a.m.   Dept.: 3   Room:

THE COURT FINDS

2. All notices required by law have been given.

3. Decedent died on *(date):* 6/1/89
   a. [X] a resident of the California county named above.
   b. [ ] a nonresident of California and left an estate in the county named above.
   c. [ ] intestate [X] testate.

THE COURT FURTHER FINDS AND ORDERS

4. a. [X] The property described in attachment 4a is property passing to the surviving spouse
      (name): JANE LONGERHERE   , and no administration of it is necessary
   b. [ ] See attachment 4b for further order respecting transfer of the property to the surviving spouse.

5. [ ] To protect the interests of the creditors of *(business name):*

      an unincorporated trade or business, a list of all its known creditors and the amount owed each is on file.
      a. [ ] Within *(specify)*   days from this date, the surviving spouse shall file an undertaking in the amount of
                     $, upon condition that the surviving spouse pay the known creditors of the business.
      b. [ ] See attachment 5b for further order protecting the interests of creditors of the business.

6. a. [X] The property described in attachment 6a is property that belongs to the surviving spouse,
      (name): JANE LONGERHERE   , under Probate Code sections 100 and 101, and the surviving
      spouse's ownership is hereby confirmed.
   b. [ ] See attachment 6b for further order respecting transfer of the property to the surviving spouse.

7. [ ] All property described in the Spousal Property Petition that is not determined to be property passing to the surviving spouse,
      under Probate Code section 13500, or confirmed as belonging to the surviving spouse under Probate Code sections 100
      and 101, shall be subject to administration in the estate [ ] described in attachment 7.

8. [ ] Other *(specify):*

Date:

9. [ ] Number of pages attached:

JUDGE OF THE SUPERIOR COURT
[X] Signature follows last attachment

Form Approved by the
Judicial Council of California
DE-226 [Rev. July 1, 1987]

SPOUSAL PROPERTY ORDER
(PROBATE)

Probate Code, § 13656

Form 14, Page 1
Spousal Property Order

SHORT TITLE: ESTATE OF N. O. LONGERHERE, DECEASED	CASE NUMBER: 10000

1 ATTACHMENT TO SPOUSAL PROPERTY ORDER.

2   Attachment 4a - Property Passing to the Surviving Spouse:

3 A one-half (1/2) undivided community interest in the real property

4 located at 10 Best Place, Heavenly, California 90000, legally

5 described as follows:

6

7 Lot 101 in Block 5, as Designated on the map entitled "Heavenly

8 Ranchos, Heavenly, California", which map was filed in the office of

9 the Recorder of the County of Comfort, State of California, on

10 February 29, 1942, in Volume 26 of Maps, at page 916.

11

12   Attachment 6a - Property Belonging to the Surviving Spouse:

13

14 A one-half (1/2) undivided community interest in the real property

15 located at 10 Best Place, Heavenly, California 90000, legally

16 described as follows:

17

18 Lot 101 in Block 5, as Designated on the map entitled "Heavenly

19 Ranchos, Heavenly, California", which map was filed in the office of

20 the Recorder of the County of Comfort, State of California, on

21 February 29, 1942, in Volume 26 of Maps, at page 916.

22

23 DATED: _____

24   JUDGE OF THE SUPERIOR COURT

25

26 *(Required for verified pleading) The items on this page stated on information and belief (specify item numbers, not line numbers):*

27 This page may be used with any Judicial Council form or any other paper filed with this court.   Page_____

Form Approved by the
Judicial Council of California
MC-020 [New January 1, 1987]

ADDITIONAL PAGE
Attach to Judicial Council Form or Other Court Paper

CRC 201, 501

Form 14, Page 2
Spousal Property Order

NOTES

Chapter 10

Personal Property, Leasehold Interests, Options and Contracts

 While acting as the real estate agent for an estate, you may also run across sales of personal property, leasehold interests, options and contracts.

Personal Property

This chapter covers sales of personal property when there is a sale of real property also involved.

Necessity for Appraisal.

If you have personal property to be included with the sale of real property, ask the attorney for the representative if the items have been appraised and the appraised value(s). More than likely, if the real property has been appraised, the personal property has also been appraised. In order to get the best price, you need to know the appraised value. The sale of tangible personal property will ordinarily not be approved unless the property has been appraised. (Probate Code Section 10005.)

Personal property can be sold with real property as a unit and under one bid, even though they have been appraised separately. However, if appraised separately, the property must be sold for not less than 90% of its appraisal. If appraised as a unit, the unit must be sold for not less than 90% of its appraisal. (Probate Code Section 10004.)

Commissions.

Commissions on sales of tangible personal property will be allowed only to individuals holding a broker's license authorizing them to deal in the type of property involved. A commission will be allowed on the original bid only when the commission is requested in the report of sale of property. (See Chapter 5.)

When there is an overbid in court, a commission may be allowed to the successful broker, and, if the original bid was subject to a commission, apportionment between the brokers will be made according to the same rules as prescribed for real estate sales. The amount of the commission is within the court's discretion and will not ordinarily exceed 10% of the sale price. (See Chapter 5 for a discussion of the commission and dividing it between brokers.)

Leasehold Interests

Sales of leasehold real property are treated as sales of personal property, except in the following instances, which are treated like real property:

- A leasehold which will run more than 10 years. (Probate Code Section 10203[b][1].)

- A leasehold interest which includes an option to purchase the leased property. (Probate Code Section 10203[b][2].)

- A lease consisting of oil or gas interests. (Probate Code Section 10203[b][3].)

If the lease is of the type noted in the three exceptions listed above, read on.

If the representative has IAEA powers, the procedures can be abbreviated. Read Chapter 2 on the Independent Administration of Estates Act.

If the representative does not have IAEA powers or the attorney for the representative decides that court approval is warranted, then a petition must be filed with the court. The hearing of the petition is about three to four weeks from the date the petition is filed. The attorney will send notice of the hearing to all interested parties. Contact the attorney a day or two before the hearing date to see if the petition is on the pre-approved list. Also ask the attorney when the signed order will be available (the time period varies from court to court).

Option to Purchase Real Property

An executor or administrator may grant an option to purchase real property to run during the period of administration of the probate or even after the probate closes. (Probate Code Section 9980.)

If the representative has IAEA powers, the procedures can be abbreviated. Read Chapter 2 on the Independent Administration of Estates Act.

If the representative does not have IAEA powers or the attorney for the representative decides that court approval is warranted, then before the representative can sign the option, a petition must be filed with the court. The purchase price must be at least 90% of the appraised value. The appraisal must be made within one year prior to the hearing of the petition.

The attorney will need the following information to prepare the petition:

- Description of the property, both street address and legal;
- Terms and conditions of the proposed option;
- Why the option is to the advantage of the estate.

The hearing of the petition is about three to four weeks from the date the petition is filed. The attorney will send notice of the hearing to all interested parties. Contact the attorney a day or two before the hearing date to see if the petition is on the pre-approved list. Also ask the attorney when the signed order will be available (the time period varies from court to court).

Contract to Purchase Real Property

The representative may sell a contract to purchase real property which the decedent owned at the time of death. (Probate Code Section 10206.)

If the representative has IAEA powers, the procedures can be abbreviated. Read Chapter 2 on the Independent Administration of Estates Act.

If the representative does not have IAEA powers or the attorney for the representative decides that court approval is warranted, then before the representative can sell the contract, a petition must be filed with the court. The attorney will need a copy of the proposed sales contract to prepare the petition.

The hearing of the petition is about three to four weeks from the date the petition is filed. The attorney will send notice of the hearing to all interested parties. Contact the attorney a day or two before the hearing date to see if the petition is on the pre-approved list. Also ask the attorney when the signed order will be available (the time period varies from court to court).

NOTES

Conservatorship

Chapter 11

Conservatorships and Guardianships

Conservatorships and guardianships also come under the jurisdiction of the probate court, and many of the procedures and terms are similar to a probate case. If you have handled probate sales, you will also be familiar with the requirements for these situations.

However, there are some differences. A probate lasts for a relatively short period and results in the estate being distributed to the heirs or beneficiaries. A conservatorship (for an adult who is incompetent to manage his or her affairs) or a guardianship (for a minor) may go on for many years. A conservatorship ends when the person regains his or her ability to handle his or her affairs or dies. A guardianship ends when the minor reaches legal adulthood.

By knowing the basic procedures you can better assist the guardian/conservator. It's important to be sure the guardian/conservator does not take action before court approval is obtained, in most instances.

The conservator/guardian may sell personal or real property for any of the following reasons (Probate Code Section 2541):

- The estate has insufficient income to take care of the conservatee/minor ward.
- There are debts over and above the available cash which must be paid.
- It is to the advantage of the estate or the conservatee/minor ward that the property be sold.

The court prefers, though, that every effort be made to keep the conservatee in his or her home as long as is physically and financially possible. The court will scrutinize the sale of a conservatee's residence very carefully to make sure there is a definite need for the sale.

Sale procedures in a guardianship or conservatorship are generally the same as in the probate estate of a person who died without a Will and an administrator has been appointed as personal representative. The powers under the Independent Administration of Estates Act (IEAE) cannot be used. Therefore, *all sales in a guardianship/conservatorship require court approval with the exception of personal property*, which we will discuss later.

Restrictions and/or Additional Powers of Guardian/Conservator.

If the conservator/guardian's powers are restricted in any way, such restrictions or conditions will be set forth as an attachment to the Letters of Conservatorship or Letters of Guardianship, which are the legal documents proving that the conservator/guardian has been appointed. (Probate Code Section 2594.) You may wish to ask the personal representative to show you the Letters of Guardianship or Conservatorship.

When the guardianship/conservatorship is instituted, or later, the guardian/conservator can ask the court for additional independent exercise of powers, such as the power to:

- Grant and take options;
- Sell real or personal property;
- Purchase real or personal property;
- Lease property;
- Exchange property; or
- Sell property on credit (note and deed of trust) if a portion of the selling price is adequately secured.

If one of these powers is granted, it is not necessary to go through the process of court petition and confirmation for that particular transaction. However, additional powers are not easily granted. The court usually prefers that the guardian/conservator ask the court's approval at the time the action is being considered (Probate Code Section 2591).

Guardianship

Appointment of Temporary Guardian/Conservator.

Some situations may necessitate the appointment of a temporary conservator or temporary guardian. Since the appointment is considered not to be permanent, a temporary conservator/guardian has considerably less discretion to sell the property of a conservatee or minor ward.

For example, in order to sell the conservatee's residence, a temporary conservator has to show that the conservatee will be unable to return to the home and that, if the property is not sold, irreparable harm to the conservatee would result. The conservatee has to be given full notice. In order to sell other real property, the temporary conservator must also show that the sale averts irreparable harm.

Case Studies

Sarah S. has Alzheimer's disease. She has no close relatives, so a conservator was found through her attorney. As the disease progressed, her doctor advised that she would need to be cared for in a nursing home, and would not be able to return to her residence. A buyer was found for the house, and the conservator petitioned the court for confirmation of the sale, showing the necessity. The court approved the sale. The proceeds were used to pay for her nursing home care.

Brian G.'s parents were divorced. His father died in a car accident when Brian was twelve, naming Brian as his only beneficiary in his Will. The primary asset in the father's estate was a small apartment building. Brian's mother petitioned to be appointed guardian of Brian's estate, and the guardianship was granted. She managed the apartment building for several years. Then, as Brian neared college age, she wanted to sell it and use the proceeds for his higher education. She listed it with a broker and a potential buyer made an offer. She petitioned the court for confirmation and the court approved the sale.

Sales of Real Property

Court approval is specifically required when real property is sold. It follows then that the terms of sale must be approved by the court. Examples of credit terms might include cash down payment and the balance subject to a note or deed of trust (amount and term), the interest rate, monthly payments and due dates, late payment charges, due-on-sale clauses, and perhaps special requirements such as a smoke alarm.

The court will, of course, be looking after the conservatee's/minor ward's best interests and will carefully review the terms of sale and credit of the purchaser. The court will also be concerned that sufficient cash and/or security has been included so little opportunity will exist for the purchaser to default on the note. (Probate Code Section 2542.)

Sale Procedures.

The procedures are discussed fully in chapters 3-5; also see the checklist at the end. As there are a few differences, we'll give a brief summary here.

The first question to ask the conservator or guardian is whether their powers are restricted in any way or whether they have any additional powers granted by the court. If they are fortunate enough to have the power to sell real property, then the sale can proceed pretty much like any other sale. However, more than likely, they will not and it will be necessary to obtain court authority to list the property.

Before the listing agreement is signed, you need to determine whether there is any personal property to be included with the sale, and check the appraised value. It is necessary that the sale price submitted to the court be at least 90% of the appraised value, using the same method of figuring as in probate sales. Also check with the attorney to see if there are any notice requirements and, if so, if they have been fulfilled.

The listing agreement should be exclusive, to assure your commission, and contain the words, "sale subject to court confirmation."

When the property has been exposed to the market and an acceptable offer has been made, you should obtain a deposit check for at least 10% of the amount bid, with the check made payable to the conservator/guardian. It should read: payable to [name]_____, [conservator/guardian] of the Estate of [name of conservatee or ward]. A copy of the deposit receipt should be sent to the attorney.

Since 10% of the purchase price will be a substantial sum of money tied up while waiting for the hearing, it will help to be able to tell the potential buyer that the money will be kept in a separate, interest-bearing account and that, if an overbidder is successful, the interest as well as the original amount will be returned. You may want to add the following wording to the deposit receipt:

Cash deposit to be placed in a separate interest-bearing account. In the event this sale is not consummated because of a successful overbid in court, principal and accrued interest to be returned to the unsuccessful bidder named herein.

The attorney will prepare the Report of Sale and Petition for Order Confirming Sale of Real Property, and the court will schedule a hearing. Be sure that you, the potential buyer, and any other broker involved attend the hearing.

At the hearing, the court will entertain overbids, just as in a probate sale. The overbid formula is also the same: the first overbid must exceed the original bid by 10% of the first $10,000 and 5% of the excess. Bidding will proceed in set increments, determined by the court.

At the end of the hearing, if all goes smoothly, the court will confirm the sale and determine the commission and its division, if more than one broker is involved.

Be sure that the escrow company sends the attorney for the conservator/guardian a copy of the escrow instructions. The attorney will provide to the escrow company a certified copy of the Order Confirming Sale, and the signed Conservator's or Guardian's Deed.

All that's left is for escrow to close, and for you to receive your commission check!

Sales of Personal Property

A conservator or guardian may sell personal property without a court order if the total of all sales made during any calendar year does not exceed $5,000 (Probate Code Section

2545).

The conservatee must consent to the sale. Of course, if the conservatee lacks "legal capacity," he or she cannot consent.

In the case of a guardianship, if the minor ward is over 14 years of age, he or she must consent to the sale. (Probate Code Section 2545[1].)

Other Real Estate Transactions

Exchanges of Real Property.

In some instances it might be beneficial for your client, the conservator/guardian, to exchange real property. A court order is necessary. The attorney will prepare a petition for the conservator/guardian, showing the court that the exchange is for the advantage, benefit and best interests of the conservatee or ward, and notice will be given to the necessary people.

Leasing of Real Property.

If you are handling the lease of real property for your client, a guardian or conservator, then you should know that the conservator/guardian may sign a lease affecting real property belonging to the estate only after court authorization. There is an exception — no court approval is necessary if:

- The rental does not exceed $1,500 per month and the term is no longer than two years; or
- The lease is from month-to-month.

If court authorization for a lease is needed, contact the attorney for the conservator/guardian. He or she will prepare the petition. The attorney will need a description of the property, the terms, and any rental or general conditions.

Sale of Leasehold Interests.

A sale of leasehold interests must conform to the procedures for sale of real property when:

- The leasehold has an unexpired term of 10 years or longer;
- The leasehold is coupled with an option to purchase the leased premises or some portion of the leased premises; or
- The leasehold consists of oil or gas leasehold interests, regardless of the term of lease.

Sale of Partnership Interests.

You may have a guardian/conservator client where there is real property in the name of a partnership. Most written partnership agreements have specific provisions for sale. The partnership agreement may impose some limitations on sale, such as a right of first refusal.

Since a partnership interest is considered personal property, as opposed to real property, court approval may be in the form of a petition for authority to transfer personal property instead of a petition to confirm the sale of real property.

Purchase of Real Property.

When real property is purchased by the guardian or conservator, the title can be held as an undivided interest, tenancy in common, community property or joint tenancy. A court order is necessary.

A guardian/conservator can invest estate funds to:

- Buy a home for the conservatee/minor ward.

- Buy a home for the person(s) the conservatee/minor ward is legally responsible to support. While a minor ward usually is not responsible for anyone else, a conservatee might be responsible for a spouse and/or minor children.

Before you ask the conservator/guardian to sign on the dotted line of a deposit receipt committing the estate to a sale, make sure the words "subject to court approval" are added to the sale offer and the conservator/guardian has discussed the proposed purchase with the attorney for the estate. The attorney will prepare a petition authorizing the purchase. The petition should also ask the court for direction to execute all the necessary documents and commitments to complete the sale transaction. Contact the attorney to make sure he has sufficient information to prepare the petition.

Joint Ventures.

A guardian/conservator may enter into a joint venture with a spouse of the conservatee or with any other person. A court order is necessary.

In a conservatorship, with court approval, a real property partial interest may be purchased by the conservator. The purchase can be with the conservatee's spouse or any other person(s). The manner of purchasing the property can be in severalty, in common, in community, or in joint tenancy. The terms can be for all cash or part cash and part credit. The petition authorizing the purchase should also ask the court for direction to execute all the necessary documents and commitments to complete the sale transaction. Contact the attorney to make sure he has sufficient information to prepare the petition.

The deposit receipt should state that the purchase is subject to court approval and confirmation. The court approval procedures are the same as in a decedent's estate. (See Chapter 5.)

NOTES

Chapter 12

Trusts

 Trusts are a different breed from a decedent's estate, a conservatorship or a guardianship. Usually court approval is not necessary in a sale or purchase involving a trust, but there may be a legal requirement to give notice to certain interested individuals. Consult the trustee's attorney so that notice, if necessary, can be given *before* you proceed.

Living (Inter Vivos) and Testamentary Trusts

It is very common now for property to be held in the name of a trust. It might be a testamentary trust or a living trust (called an inter vivos trust in legal terminology). There are other kinds of trusts but we shall limit this book to exploring only these two.

A testamentary trust will result when a person in his or her Will leaves all or a portion of his or her estate to a named person "in trust" for that person to manage and take care of for the benefit of someone else.

A living, or inter vivos, trust is created and operates while the person who created it is alive. The trustor (person making the trust) is usually the same as the trustee (person who manages the trust estate). Then when the trustor dies, the alternate trustee named in the trust agreement will manage the property, in the manner specified in the agreement and according to California laws governing trusts.

The Trustee

The trustee is responsible for the estate. In order to be more professional in your service, you should know some basic things about a trust and the trustee's responsibilities.

The trustee must handle the trust according to the written trust instrument. The California Probate Code also sets forth rules which the trustee must abide by. The trustee must manage the trust estate solely for the benefit of the beneficiaries. The trustee cannot profit from the trust and has a duty to take reasonable steps to control and preserve the trust property and to make it productive. Also the trustee has the power to dispose of useless property. (Probate Code Sections 16000-16008.)

The California Probate Code sets out a standard of care to which the trustee must adhere. The trustee must also keep the beneficiaries of the trust reasonably informed of the administration and periodically make an accounting to them. (Probate Code Sections 16040-16064.)

Powers of the Trustee.

Some of the trustee's powers dealing with real estate which you, as a real estate agent or broker, should know are:

- Power to acquire or dispose of property, for cash or on credit, at public or private sale, or by exchange.

- Power to manage property, more specifically, to control, divide, develop, improve, exchange, partition, change the character of, or abandon trust property or any interest in trust property.

- Power to encumber or mortgage property.

- Power to make repairs, alterations or improvements.

- Power to demolish any improvements.

- Power to subdivide or develop land.

- Power to enter into or renew a lease.

- Power to enter into a lease or arrangement for exploration and removal of gas, oil or other minerals.

- Power to grant or take options on trust property.

- Power to insure trust property against damage.
- Power to pay taxes and assessments.
- Power to distribute property.

Liability of the Trustee.

If a trustee is at fault while handling trust property, he or she may be personally liable, so it is important that you coordinate any sale or purchase with the trustee and the trustee's attorney. Remember, it may be necessary to give notice first. (Probate Code Section 18001.)

NOTES

Chapter 13

Prospecting for Probate Sales

 Now that you have purchased and read this book, and have it available in the event you are involved in a probate sale, you have an advantage over other real estate agents or brokers. Many agents shy away from probate sales, or at least do not actively pursue them, because they are uncertain about the court procedures and paperwork. However, you now know the ins and outs of probate sales and are qualified to be a specialist. You may very well be the only one in your office who knows how to do them properly.

Your next question is going to be how you can find out who has property in probate who might need your services, which, if you help sell the property, will put money in your pocket.

The following are some ways in which you can prospect for probate sales.

Check Legal Notices in Newspapers

There are two notices which will appear in your local newspapers, in the legal advertising, which is generally found at the beginning of the classified ads section. If your community is large enough, there may also be a legal newspaper and it would be well worth the investment to subscribe to it.

The Notice of Petition to Administer Estate.

The Notice of Petition to Administer Estate is the first notice published when a probate is opened. It notifies the public that the person is deceased, that an individual has applied to be the personal representative, and advises creditors how to file claims. You can't tell from the Notice of Petition to Administer Estate whether the estate contains real property which will be sold, but it's certainly worth checking. See Form 17 at the end of this chapter for a sample of the Notice of Petition to Administer Estate.

The Notice of Sale of Real Property at Private Sale.

If you remember from Chapter 3, if the Will did not contain a power of sale clause or there was no Will, then the first step in listing property is to publish a Notice of Sale of Real Property at Private Sale. There may or may not be a listing broker by this time. But you definitely know that there is real property to be sold and can pursue either acquiring the listing or finding a prospective buyer to bid on the property.

The name and address of the attorney for the representative are listed in the notice(s). A proposed letter to the attorney is as follows:

Dear Attorney:

Re: _____ Estate

I notice from reading the Notice of Petition to Administer Estate (or Notice of Sale of Real Property at Private Sale) in the _____ newspaper that you are the attorney for the executor/administrator ____[name]____.

In the event there is real property in this estate which must be sold during probate, I would appreciate the opportunity to discuss with you the estate's needs for a listing agent/broker.

I am familiar with probate sales. My commitment is to provide expertise in real estate probate sales, to effectively advertise and market the property and then close the sale as expeditiously as possible.

I will be responsive and pay personal attention to your client's needs.

Let me discuss this matter with you at your earliest convenience.

Very truly yours,

(Your Name)
(Your Agency)

Form 15
Proposed Prospecting Letter to Attorney

I suggest that you send a letter each time you read a Notice of Petition to Administer Estate in a newspaper. In this computerized era, it's easy to set up such a form letter on a computer and then just fill in the specific information. It may be that the particular estate that you are writing the letter about does not have any property to be sold, but you will have continuously put your name before the attorney and perhaps, in a future probate sale, he will remember you.

Check Petition for Probate at the Courthouse

The court and case number are listed in the Notice of Petition to Administer Estate or Notice of Sale of Real Property at Private Sale. Go to the county clerk's office, probate section, and ask to look at the file. The fact that there is real property in the estate and the approximate value will be stated on the first page at item 3c. The proposed representative's name will be stated in item 2b. Sometimes the address of the personal representative will be listed at item 8. If it is not listed, then send a letter to the representative in care of the attorney. More than likely the attorney will forward your letter to the representative unopened. A form of proposed letter to the representative is as follows:

Dear _____ *:*

      Re: _____ *Estate*

     I notice from reading the Notice of Petition to Administer Estate (or Notice of Sale of Real Property at Private Sale) in the _____ *newspaper that you are the executor/administrator of the above-mentioned estate.*

     In the event there is real property in this estate which must be sold during probate, I would appreciate the opportunity to discuss with you listing the property.

     I am familiar with probate sales. My commitment is to provide expertise in listing and selling real estate in probate, to effectively advertise and market the property and then close the sale as expeditiously as possible.

     I will be responsive and pay personal attention to your needs.

     Let me discuss this matter with you at your earliest convenience.

     Very truly yours,

     (Your Name)
     (Your Agency)

Form 16
Proposed Prospecting Letter to Representative

You may also be able to tell from the multiple listing whether the property is a probate sale, depending on how your local multiple listing service handles this.

You can also keep an eye out for sales of property in conservatorship and guardianship cases. Notices of sales of both real and personal property are posted at the Superior Court in each county.

Of course, it's not necessary to acquire the listing to make a commission on a probate sale. Just look over your list of clients looking for property and see how many of them you can match to the probate property.

This is a great opportunity to expand your client list, particularly to include real estate investors. Probate property is ideal, because it can often be purchased below, at, or close to the appraised value. Sometimes it falls into the fixer-upper category, particularly if it has been owned by elderly people who could not provide the upkeep and improvements needed. A little sprucing up and modernization, and it can be sold for considerably more than the purchase price.

Happy prospecting!

NOTICE OF PETITION TO ADMINISTER ESTATE OF
N.O. LONGERHERE
CASE NO. 10000

To all heirs, beneficiaries, creditors, contingent creditors, and persons who may otherwise be interested in the will or estate, or both, of N. O. LONGERHERE.

A PETITION has been filed by I.M. STANDIN in the Superior Court of California, County of Comfort.

THE PETITION requests that: I.M. STANDIN be appointed as personal representative to administer the estate of the decedent.

THE PETITION requests the decedent's WILL and codicils, if any, be admitted to probate. The will and any codicils are available for examination in the file kept by the court.

THE PETITION requests authority to administer the estate under the Independent Administration of Estates Act. (This authority will allow the personal representative to take many actions without obtaining court approval. Before taking certain very important actions, however, the personal representative will be required to give notice to interested persons unless they have waived notice or consented to the proposed action.) The independent administration authority will be granted unless an interested person files an objection to the petition and shows good cause why the court should not grant the authority.

A HEARING on the petition will be held on July 15, 1989, at 9:00 a.m., in Dept. 3, located at the Court Building, Heavenly, California.

IF YOU OBJECT to the granting of the petition, you should appear at the hearing and state your objections or file written objections with the court before the hearing. Your appearance may be in person or by your attorney.

IF YOU ARE A CREDITOR or a contingent creditor of the deceased, you must file your claim with the court and mail a copy to the personal representative appointed by the court within four months from the date of first issuance of letters as provided in section 9100 of the California Probate Code. The time for filing claims will not expire before four months from the hearing date noticed above.

YOU MAY EXAMINE the file kept by the court. If you are a person interested in the estate, you may file with the court a formal Request for Special Notice of the filing of an inventory and appraisal of estate assets or of any petition or account as provided in section 1250 of the California Probate Code. A Request for Special Notice form is available from the court clerk.

JOHN Q. LAWYER
Attorney for petitioner:
JOHN Q. LAWYER
100 City Justice Building, Suite 200, Heavenly, CA 90000

Sample provided by the Daily Journal Corp., California's largest publisher of legal newspapers.

Form 17
Notice of Petition to Administer Estate

NOTES

Checklist: Probate

BEFORE THE LISTING AGREEMENT IS SIGNED:

The Personal Representative has full IAEA powers. Circle: Yes   No.

If:

_____ The Will contains a power of sale clause, or, if the Will does not contain a power of sale clause and the Notice of Sale of Real Property at Private Sale has been published; **and**

_____ You have checked to see if any personal property is to be included in the sale; **and**

_____ You have checked the probate referee's appraisal (amount of appraisal $_____); **and**

_____ You have called the attorney for the personal representative to make sure the Notice of Proposed Action re intent to list property has been mailed to all interested persons, if necessary; **and**

_____ The Order for Exclusive Listing Agreement has been obtained, if the representative does not have _full_ IAEA powers or you want to be assured the commission;

then:

You are ready to request the representative to sign the Listing Agreement and proceed with the sale.

LISTING AGREEMENT:

_____ Listing Agreement exclusive to assure commission. Circle: Yes No.

_____ Listing agreement contains words *"Sale subject to court confirmation"* or , if sold under the IAEA, *"Sale subject to consent of all heirs or beneficiaries or subject to court confirmation."*

_____ *Date Listing Agreement signed* _____.

_____ *Date Listing Agreement expires* _____. *(Mark this date on your calendar; see Chapter 4 for what to do when agreement about to expire.)*

ACCEPTING AN OFFER:

_____ Property has been properly exposed.

_____ Terms of sale are consistent with Notice of Sale of Real Property at Private Sale (if a notice was published).

_____ Amount bid is 90% of the court appraised value. (What constitutes a 90% bid may differ from county to county.)

_____ Deposit check is for at least 10% of the amount bid. Check made payable to the personal representative: [name], [executor/administrator] of the Estate of [decedent], Deceased.

_____ Deposit receipt signed. Date: _____.

_____ Copy of deposit receipt sent to attorney for representative; and attorney notified of efforts to expose property.

_____ Hearing on Report of Sale and Petition for Order Confirming Sale of Real Property. Date: _____. (Put on your calendar and plan to attend, along with your buyer.)

_____ Bid confirmed by court. Commission of $_____ ordered.

OPENING THE ESCROW:

_____ Escrow opened. Date: _____.

_____ Escrow requested to send attorney for representative a copy of escrow instructions.

_____ Escrow scheduled to close. Date: _____.

CLOSING THE ESCROW:

_____ Certified copy of Order Confirming Sale sent to the escrow.

_____ Executed Executor's/Administrator's Deed sent to escrow.

_____ Escrow closed. Date: _____.

_____ Commission check received.

Checklist:
Conservatorship/Guardianship

BEFORE THE LISTING AGREEMENT IS SIGNED:

_____ Conservator/guardian has additional powers relating to real estate. Circle: Yes No.
They are:_____.

If:

_____ You have checked to see if any personal property is to be included in the sale; .
and

_____ You have checked the probate referee appraisal (amount of appraisal $_____);
and

_____ You have checked with the attorney to be sure that any requirements for notice have been fulfilled;

then:

You are ready to request the conservator/guardian to sign the Listing Agreement and proceed with the sale.

LISTING AGREEMENT:

_____ Listing Agreement exclusive to assure commission. Circle: Yes No.

_____ Listing agreement contains words "sale subject to court confirmation."

_____ Date Listing Agreement signed _____.

_____ Date Listing Agreement expires _____.
(Mark this date on your calendar; see Chapter 4 for what to do when agreement about to expire.)

ACCEPTING AN OFFER:

_____ Property has been properly exposed.

_____ Amount bid is 90% of the court appraised value.

_____ Deposit check is for at least 10% of the amount bid.

_____ Check made payable to the conservator/guardian: [name], conservator/guardian] of the Estate of [name], conservatee/ward.

_____ Deposit receipt signed. Date: _____.

_____ Copy of deposit receipt sent to attorney for conservator/guardian; and attorney notified of efforts to expose property.

_____ Hearing on Report of Sale and Petition for Order Confirming Sale of Real Property. Date:_____. (Put on your calendar and plan to attend, along with your buyer.)

_____ Bid confirmed by court. Commission of $_____ ordered.

OPENING THE ESCROW:

_____ Escrow opened. Date: _____.

_____ Escrow requested to send attorney for conservator/guardian a copy of escrow instructions.

_____ Escrow scheduled to close. Date: _____.

CLOSING THE ESCROW:

_____ Certified copy of Order Confirming Sale sent to the escrow.

_____ Executed Conservator's/Guardian's Deed sent to escrow.

_____ Escrow closed. Date: _____.

_____ Commission check received.

Checklist: Community Property

_____ Has 40 days passed since date of death?
Date of death: _____.
_____ Listing Agreement signed.
_____ Date: _____ (put on your calendar).
_____ Expires: _____ (put on your calendar;
see Chapter 4 for what to do when agreement about
to expire).
_____ Spousal Property Petition filed.
Hearing date: _____ (put on your calendar).
_____ Spousal Property Petition granted. (Check with attorney the day before the hearing.)
_____ Certified copy of Spousal Property Order given to escrow.
_____ Escrow closed.
_____ Commission check received.

Appendix

Local Court Rules on Sales

It is suggested that you review the local court rules for the county in which you have a sale. The rules included in this section are particular to each county. Rules common in all counties have not been listed. Common sense indicates that some of these rules should apply in all counties, but some counties are more fussy than others about a given situation.

ALAMEDA COUNTY

1. Exclusive Listings: Petitions for exclusive listings will be granted only where a clear showing of necessity and advantage to the estate is made.

The petition and proposed order should include:

a. That the court sets commissions and that they are due only if the sale is confirmed;

b. That duplicate commissions are not payable should there be a successful overbid in court; and

c. The duration of the contract (ordinarily the court will not approve a term exceeding 90 days).

A copy of the listing agreement should be attached to the petition for an exclusive listing. The listing agreement must correspond to the conditions set forth above and additionally set forth in detail the obligations and duties of the broker, including, but not limited to, the requirement to list on multiple listing service(s), place signs and advertise in newspaper(s).

Extensions of listing agreements should comply with the above procedures. Rule 809.

2. Broker's Commission:

a. **Improved Real Property:** Ordinarily not to exceed 6%. Rule 803.1.

b. **Unimproved Real Property:** Ordinarily not to exceed 10% of the first $20,000, 8% of the next $30,000 and 5% of the balance of the sales price. Rule 803.2.

c. **Ordinarily no commission for brokers bidding or overbidding on their own behalf.** Rule 803.3.

3. The Court will not consider whether a broker is employed when receiving overbids. Rule 803.4.

4. Division of Commissions:

a. When a broker represents the original bidder and another agent brings in a successful overbid: one-half of the commission on the original bid to the original broker and the remaining one-half the commission on the original bid plus all of the commission on the overbid amount to the successful overbidding broker.

b. No broker on the original bid, but a broker represents the successful overbid: broker for successful overbidder allowed one-half of a full commission on the amount of the original bid and a full commission on the difference between the original bid and the increased bid.

c. A broker on the original bid, but no broker on the successful overbid: original broker allowed the full commission on the original amount bid.

d. In no case may the commission of the broker for an increased successful bidder exceed one-half of the difference between the amount bid in the original return and the amount of the successful bid; however, this limitation does not apply to the agent holding the listing agreement with the personal representative. Rule 803.5

5. **Cash Deposit to Accompany Bid:** Bids shall be accompanied by a minimum of 10% of amount bid. When an overbid is made in Court, the bidder shall submit cash, money order or certified check at the time of the hearing in the amount of 10% of the minimum overbid. (See Chapter 5 to figure minimum overbid.) Rule 804.

6. **If the property is being sold subject to an encumbrance, the published notice of sale should so state.** Rule 806.

7. Report of Sale and Petition for Order Confirming Sale of Real Property: All extraordinary costs, such as termite and other repairs, lender's points, loan fees and nonrecurring closing costs, should be disclosed in the petition for confirmation of sale. Check the petition to make sure it is accurate. Rule 807.1.

Extraordinary costs, such as termite and other repairs, lender's points, loan fees and nonrecurring closing costs, will be used to:

a. Determine if the sale is at least 90% of the appraised value.

b. Determine the base figure from which overbids are made.

c. Determine the real estate broker's commission.

The following are examples of how to figure the net:

Appraised value $210,000

Example 1: Gross bid $200,000
Deduct all expenses of sale   (650)
          Net bid   199,350
90% of $210,000 = $189,000
The net bid of $199,350 would be within 90% of the appraised value.

Example 2: Gross bid $189,000
Deduct all expenses of sale   (650)
          Net bid   188,350
90% of $210,000 = $189,000
The net bid of $188,350 would *not* be at least 90% of the appraised value.

The amounts listed in items a, b, and c should be set out in the report of sale and petition for order confirming sale, so check the petition to make sure it is correct.

8. Sales of Mobile Homes, Cooperatives, Timeshare Units and Houseboats: While considered personal property, these items shall be sold according to Probate Code provisions relating to real property. Rule 815.

9. Sale of Property Specifically Bequeathed: Notice of time and place of hearing of the return of sale shall be given to the person to whom it is bequeathed, or his or her consent to such sale filed. Rule 812.

ALPINE COUNTY

1. Sale or Encumbrance of Specifically Bequeathed Property: No specifically bequeathed real or personal property shall be encumbered or offered for sale unless first approved by the court on seven court days notice to the person to whom it was bequeathed. Rule 12.14, Uniform Rules of Third District Superior Courts.

AMADOR COUNTY

1. Sale or Encumbrance of Specifically Bequeathed Property: No specifically bequeathed real or personal property shall be encumbered or offered for sale unless first approved by the court on seven court days notice to the person to whom it was bequeathed. Rule

12.14, Uniform Rules of Third District Superior Courts.

BUTTE COUNTY

1. Sale or Encumbrance of Specifically Bequeathed Property: No specifically bequeathed real or personal property shall be encumbered or offered for sale unless first approved by the court on seven court days notice to the person to whom it was bequeathed. Rule 12.14, Uniform Rules of Third District Superior Courts.

CALAVERAS COUNTY

1. Sale or Encumbrance of Specifically Bequeathed Property: No specifically bequeathed real or personal property shall be encumbered or offered for sale unless first approved by the court on seven court days notice to the person to whom it was bequeathed. Rule 12.14, Uniform Rules of Third District Superior Courts.

COLUSA COUNTY

1. Sale or Encumbrance of Specifically Bequeathed Property: No specifically bequeathed real or personal property shall be encumbered or offered for sale unless first approved by the court on seven court days notice to the person to whom it was bequeathed. Rule

12.14, Uniform Rules of Third District Superior Courts.

CONTRA COSTA COUNTY

1. Cash Deposit: Bids must be accompanied by a minimum deposit of 10% of the purchase price unless the loan proceeds exceed 90% of the purchase price. Rule 501(a).

2. Market Exposure to Property: If it is brought to the attention of the court that the representative has denied bona fide prospective buyers or their brokers a reasonable opportunity to inspect the property, the returned sale will not be confirmed, and the sale will be continued to allow inspection. Rule 501(b).

3. Second Deeds of Trust: The court will approve the taking of a promissory note secured by a junior deed of trust upon a showing that it serves the best interests of the estate. Rule 501(c).

4. Application of Statutory Formula re Overbid: The court must consider not only whether the bid is arithmetically the highest, but also whether it is the best. The court may ask to see factual information to substantiate the bid. Rule 501(d).

5. Ernest Money Deposit by Increase Bidder: The successful overbidder must submit at the hearing a certified or cashier's check for 10% of the bid, but not to exceed the amount of the cash down payment, plus the overbid. Rule 501(e).

6. Broker's Commission — General Rule:

a. Improved Property: The court will ordinarily allow a broker's commission not to exceed 6% of the first $100,000, 5% of the next $50,000, and 4% of the balance of the sales price. The parties may agree to a lesser percentage. Rule 502(b).

For Example:

If the sales price was $200,000:

6% of the first $100,000	$ 6,000
5% of the next 50,000	2,500
4% of the balance of 50,000	2,000
Total commission court will ordinarily allow	$ 10,500

b. Unimproved Property: In the court's discretion, a flat 10% may be allowed; but the court will ordinarily allow a broker's commission not to exceed 10% of the first $30,000, 8% of the next $40,000, and 5% of the balance of the sales price. The determination as to what is unimproved real property is made by the court. Rule 502(b).

c. Commission in Excess of Schedule: Under unusual circumstances, a commission exceeding the normal schedule will be allowed. In this instance, the court would prefer that the written consent of the beneficiaries be obtained. Rule 502(d).

d. Broker Bidding for Own Account Not Entitled to a Commission: A broker bidding for his own account is not entitled to receive or share in a commission. (Estate of Toy (1977) 73 Cal. App. 3d 392.) Rule 502(e).

DEL NORTE COUNTY

There are no specific local rules on sales.

EL DORADO COUNTY

1. Sale or Encumbrance of Specifically Bequeathed Property: No specifically bequeathed real or personal property shall be encumbered or offered for sale unless first approved by the court on seven court days notice to the person to whom it was bequeathed. Rule 12.14, Uniform Rules of Third District Superior Courts.

FRESNO COUNTY

1. Brokers' Commission: (Rule 7.2.)
    a. Improved Real Property: Unless justified by exceptional circumstances, the court will not allow a broker's commission in excess of 6%.
    b. Unimproved Real Property: A commission of up to 10% may be allowed.
    c. Broker for Successful Overbidder: The court must be advised at the beginning of the hearing on the confirmation of sale and before the bidding begins that a potential overbidder is represented by a broker. If the court is not advised, the broker for the overbidder will not be allowed a commission.
    2. Assumption of Encumbrance on Sales of Real Property: The court will ordinarily not confirm a sale where the buyer assumes or

takes subject to an existing encumbrance(s) which would leave the estate subject to a contingent liability. The report of sale and petition for order confirming sale should set forth all pertinent facts so that the court can make a determination.

3. **Sales of Specifically Bequeathed Real or Personal Property:** Ten days notice of time and place of hearing of the return of sale shall be given to the person to whom it is bequeathed, unless the consent to such sale is on file.

GLENN COUNTY

There are no specific local rules on sales.

HUMBOLDT COUNTY

1. **Sale or Encumbrance of Specifically Bequeathed Property:** No specifically bequeathed real or personal property shall be encumbered or offered for sale unless first approved by the court on seven court days notice to the person to whom it was bequeathed. Rule 12.14.

IMPERIAL COUNTY

There are no specific local rules on sales.

INYO COUNTY

There are no specific local rules on sales.

KERN COUNTY

Kern County follows Los Angeles County Probate Rules.

KINGS COUNTY

There are no specific local rules on sales.

LAKE COUNTY

There are no specific local rules on sales.

LASSEN COUNTY

1. Sale or Encumbrance of Specifically Bequeathed Property: No specifically bequeathed real or personal property shall be encumbered or offered for sale unless first approved by the court on seven court days notice to the person to whom it was bequeathed. Rule 12.14, Uniform Rules of Third District Superior Courts.

LOS ANGELES COUNTY

1. Broker's Commission: The court will not allow a broker's commission in excess of 5%, unless justified by exceptional circumstances. Rule 12.05.

2. When Buyer Assumes Encumbrance: The court will ordinarily not confirm a sale where the buyer assumes or takes subject to an existing encumbrance which would leave the estate subject to a contingent liability. The report of sale and petition for order confirming sale should set forth all pertinent facts so that the court can make a determination. Rule 12.06.

3. **Sale of Specifically Bequeathed Property:** 15 days notice of time and place of hearing of the return of sale must be given to the person to whom it is bequeathed, unless his or her consent is on file with the court.

4. **Overbids:** If the bid returned for confirmation is upon credit and an overbid is either for cash or credit, whether on the same or different terms, the overbid offer shall be considered only if the personal representative, prior to the confirmation of the sale, informs the court that the offer is acceptable.

If the bid returned for confirmation is for cash and an overbid is upon credit, the overbid offer shall be considered only if the personal representative, prior to confirmation of sale, informs the court that the offer is acceptable. Rule 12.10.

5. **Increased Bid Forms:** A successful overbidder in open court must complete and sign an "Increased Bid in Open Court" form. The order for confirmation of sale will not be signed until the bid form has been filed. Rule 12.11.

6. **Sales by Guardians and Conservators:** Sales of property by guardians and conservators must be approved by the court. It is not the intention of the court to grant a conservator a special power of sale. Rule 12.12.

7. Conditional Sales of Real Property: The court will ordinarily not approve a sale of real property which is conditioned upon the occurrence of a subsequent event (such as change in zoning or obtaining approval from an environmental control board). However, if unusual and extraordinary circumstances exist and the necessity and advantage to the estate are set forth in detail, the court may approve such a sale. Rule 12.13.

8. Sale of Mobile Homes: The court will approve the sale of mobile homes as depreciating property. The petition for approval must set forth the efforts made to expose the property to the market. Rule 12.14.

MADERA COUNTY

1. Sale or Encumbrance of Estate Property: All petitions for the sale or encumbrance of estate property must be accompanied by a declaration under oath that the property is not specifically bequeathed. No specifically bequeathed real or personal property shall be encumbered or offered for sale unless first approved by the court on seven court days notice to the person to whom it is bequeathed. Rule 10.18.

MARIN COUNTY

1. Exposure to Market: The court will examine the personal representative's efforts to expose the property to the market. Rule 1000(b).

2. Notice of Sale of Real Property: Marin County prefers that if the property is being sold subject to an encumbrance the notice should so state. (See Mains v. City Title Insurance Co., (1949) 34 C2d 580.)

When a deed of trust is proposed as part of the consideration, the court will require a special showing that it is not disadvantageous for the estate to accept, as part of the purchase price, a note secured by a deed of trust. Rule 1002.

3. Sales Where Buyer Assumes Encumbrance: The court will not ordinarily confirm a sale where the buyer assumes or takes subject to an existing encumbrance unless it appears that the estate will have no further liability in connection with the encumbrance. Rule 1005.

4. Cash Deposits to Accompany Increased Bid: The overbidder must submit cash or a cashier's check at the time of the hearing for 10% of the minimum increased bid. The minimum increased bid is a bid which exceeds the sale price of the original bid by 10% of the first $10,000 and 5% of the balance of the sales price. Rule 1007.

5. Broker's Commission: Commissions will normally be allowed as set forth below. Exceptional circumstances may justify a greater allowance.

a. **Improved:** Not to exceed 6% of the first $100,000 and 5% of any excess over $100,000.

b. **Unimproved:** Not to exceed 10% of the first $20,000, 8% of the next $30,000 and 5% of the balance of the sales price. The court will make the determination if the property is unimproved. Rule 1008.

    c. Allocation: The court shall give consideration to any agreement between the broker with a written contract and any cooperating broker whose bid was returned to the court, with respect to the sharing of commission.

    6. Division of Commission If Successful Overbid:

    a. Both original bidder and successful overbidder have brokers: One-half of the commission on the original bid to go to the agent whose bid was returned to court and the balance of the commission on the purchase price to the agent who procured the successful overbidder, observing the limitation that the compensation of the broker for the overbidder shall not exceed one-half of the difference between the original bid and the overbid. Such limitation shall not apply to the agent holding the contract with the personal representative.

    b. Only original bidder has broker: Agent holding the contract allowed a full commission on the amount of the original bid returned by him.

    c. Only successful overbidder has broker: Broker receives one-half of the commission on the original bid, plus a full commission on the excess of the increased bid over the original bid, observing the limitation stated above.

    7. Only Highest and Best Offer May Be Accepted: The personal representative may accept only the highest and best offer (i.e., most favorable to the estate), whether or not it is submitted through the listing broker. Rule 1009.1(d).

8. Sale of Condominiums, Community or Cooperative Apartments: Although community or cooperative apartments are personal property (stock) coupled with a right of occupancy and may be sold as personal property (with no publication necessary), overbids on such assets will be computed on the same basis as real property and broker's commissions will be allowed on the same basis as real property.

Condominiums are interests in real property and must be sold as such. Rule 1015.

MARIPOSA COUNTY

There are no specific local rules on sales.

MENDOCINO COUNTY

There are no specific local rules on sales.

MERCED COUNTY

1. Sale or Encumbrance of Bequeathed Real Property: No specifically bequeathed real property shall be encumbered or offered for sale unless first approved by the court after not less than ten days notice to the person to whom it is bequeathed, or the consent of the person is on file. Rule 901.

2. Exclusive Listing of Real Property: A copy of the proposed agreement with the broker should be attached to the petition requesting an exclusive listing. No such agreement shall provide for the payment of a commission to the broker holding the listing in the event of sale to a buyer produced by the personal representative, although commissions will be allowed pursuant to the Probate Code in the event of increased bids in open court.

The order for the listing agreement should state that a reasonable broker's commission will be determined by the court at the time of confirmation of sale. Rule 903.

3. Broker's Commission: Upon confirmation, a broker's commission in excess of 6% of the gross sales price will not be allowed unless prior court order was obtained. Rule 907.

4. Conditional Sales of Real Property: Ordinarily the court will not approve a sale which is conditioned upon the occurrence of an ensuing event (such as change in zoning or obtaining approval from an environmental control board). If unusual and extraordinary circumstances exist and the necessity and advantage to the estate are set forth in detail, the court may approve the sale. Rule 909.

5. Sales When Buyer Assumes Encumbrance: The court will not ordinarily confirm a sale where the buyer assumes or takes subject to an existing encumbrance unless the estate will have no further liability in connection with the encumbrance. The report of sale and petition for order confirming sale should set forth the facts pertinent to such assumption agreement and any contingent liability. Rule 910.

6. Bid Form: Any overbidders will be required to fill out a blank bid form. Obtain the blank bid form from the attorney for the representative at the hearing on the confirmation of sale. Rule 911.

MODOC COUNTY

1. Sale or Encumbrance of Specifically Bequeathed Property: No specifically bequeathed real or personal property shall be encumbered or offered for sale unless first approved by the court on seven court days notice to the person to whom it was bequeathed. Rule 12.14, Uniform Rules of Third District Superior Courts.

MONO COUNTY

1. Sale or Encumbrance of Specifically Bequeathed Property: No specifically bequeathed real or personal property shall be encumbered or offered for sale unless first approved by the court on seven court days notice to the person to whom it was bequeathed. Rule 12.14, Uniform Rules of Third District Superior Courts.

MONTEREY COUNTY

1. Broker's Commission on Real Property:

a. **General Rule:** A commission which exceeds the normal schedule will be allowed only under the most unusual circumstances. In such circumstances, the court prefers that the written agreement of the beneficiaries be obtained. Rule 4.20(b).

b. Disputes About Brokers' Commissions: Normally disputes about brokers' commissions will be referred to the appropriate Board of Realtors for arbitration.

c. Appearance of Broker: If a broker claims to be entitled to a commission, that broker should appear in order to be sure he or she agrees on any splitting of commissions in the event of a successful overbid. Rule 4.20(d).

2. Commissions on Tangible Personal Property: Ordinarily the commission will not exceed 10% of the sale price. If there is an overbid in court, the commission will be apportioned between the brokers according to the same rules as real estate sales. Rule 4.22(a).

NAPA COUNTY

There are no specific local rules on sales.

NEVADA COUNTY

1. Sale or Encumbrance of Specifically Bequeathed Property: No specifically bequeathed real or personal property shall be encumbered or offered for sale unless first approved by the court on seven court days notice to the person to whom it was bequeathed. Rule 12.14, Uniform Rules of Third District Superior Courts.

ORANGE COUNTY

1. **Sale of Bequeathed Property:** On a sale of specifically bequeathed real or personal property, ten days notice of the hearing of the petition for confirmation and a copy of the petition must be given to the person to whom it is bequeathed or his consent filed. Rule 5.01.

2. **Sales of Cooperatives and Mobile Homes:** Sales of cooperatives (such as those in Leisure World) may be sold as personal property if the estate will incur loss or expense by keeping the property, or alternatively, may be sold as a security. Similarly, the court will approve sales of mobile homes as depreciating property. Such petitions will be considered by the court ex parte and appraisals will be required. Rule 5.04.

3. **Exclusive Listings:** The exclusive listing agreement should set forth in detail why the agreement is necessary and of advantage to the estate. A bare statement of "necessity and advantage" will not suffice. Rule 5.05.

4. **Brokers' Commission:** The court will not allow a broker's commission in excess of 6% unless justified by exceptional circumstances. Rule 506(a).

5. **Division of Commissions:** When a sale is confirmed to a successful overbidder who is represented by an agent, in the absence of an agreement between the listing agent and the agent representing the original bidder regarding payment of commissions in the event of a successful overbid, no compensation shall be

paid to the agent or broker who represented the unsuccessful original bidder.

The following guideline will be used:

TERMS:
No broker: buyer acting for self;
Broker: broker acting for another;
Broker-buyer: broker acting for self.

1. No broker on original bid : No commission.

    a. *No broker on overbid* : No commission.

    b. *Broker on overbid*: Up to 6% on overbid plus up to 3% on original bid.

    c. *Broker-buyer on overbid* (see note below): Up to 1% on overbid plus up to 3% on original bid.

2. Broker on original bid: If purchaser on overbid is not a broker, full commission; otherwise one-half commission on original bid.

    a. *No broker on overbid*: No commission.

    b. *Broker on overbid*: Up to 6% on overbid plus one-half commission on original bid.

    c. *Broker-buyer on overbid* (see note below): Up to 1% on overbid plus up to one-half commission on original bid.

3. Broker-buyer on original bid (see note below): Up to one-half commission on original bid.

    a. *No broker on overbid*: No commission.

b. *Broker on overbid*: Up to 6% on overbid plus one-half commission on original bid.

c. *Broker-buyer on overbid* (see note below): Up to 1% on overbid plus up to one-half commission on original bid.

NOTE: The court and parties are not bound by this guideline. Regardless of the formula, the commission on an overbid may not exceed one-half of the difference between the original bid and the successful overbid unless the broker has a contract. No commission will be allowed to a broker-buyer unless there has been full disclosure to all interested parties.

6. **Exposure to Market:** The court requires as part of the report of sale and petition for order confirming sale a declaration as to the extent and method of exposing the property to the market. If the court is not satisfied with the information contained in the petition, the judge may ask for oral testimony regarding the following questions:

- Was the property listed with a broker? If so, the type of listing. Was property placed in multiple listing?
- The extent of advertising and method (newspapers, signs, etc). If a newspaper, the number of publications.
- Number of open houses held, if any.
- Period of time property was exposed for sale.

Rule 5.06(b).

7. Terms of sale: The personal representative must inform the court prior to confirmation of sale that an offer is acceptable if:

a. The bid returned for confirmation is upon a credit, an overbid, either for cash or upon a credit, whether on the same or different credit terms; or

b. The bid returned for confirmation is for cash and an overbid is made to court which is upon a credit. Rule 5.07.

In the event of sales other than cash where it is contemplated that distribution of promissory notes, etc., will be made in kind, the court will require that the interested parties receive 10 days notice of the hearing with a copy of the petition for confirmation.

8. Conditional Sales: The court discourages sales conditioned upon the occurrence of a subsequent event, such as obtaining financing, changing zoning, or obtaining approval from an environmental control board. However, if unusual and extraordinary circumstances exist, and it is necessary and advantageous to the estate, such sales may be confirmed.

PLACER COUNTY

1. Sale or Encumbrance of Specifically Bequeathed Property: No specifically bequeathed real or personal property shall be encumbered or offered for sale unless first approved by the court on seven court days notice to the person to whom it was bequeathed. Rule

12.14, Uniform Rules of Third District Superior Courts.

PLUMAS COUNTY

1. Sale or Encumbrance of Specifically Bequeathed Property: No specifically bequeathed real or personal property shall be encumbered or offered for sale unless first approved by the court on seven court days notice to the person to whom it was bequeathed. Rule 12.14, Uniform Rules of Third District Superior Courts.

RIVERSIDE COUNTY

1. Broker's Commission:
    a. Improved: The court will not allow a broker's commission in excess of 6% unless justified by exceptional circumstances.
    b. Unimproved: The broker's commission on nonresidential real property will be set by the court on an individual basis. Where more than one broker is involved, petitioner shall indicate how the commission is to be allocated.
    Rule 6.0903.
    2. Sale of Bequeathed Property: On a sale of specifically bequeathed real or personal property, notice of the hearing must be given to the person to whom it is bequeathed, or his or her consent filed. Rule 6.0904.

SACRAMENTO COUNTY

1. **Broker's Commission:**
   a. **Improved Property:** 6%.
   b. **Unimproved Property:**
      10% on first $20,000,
      8% on next $30,000,
      5% on amount over $50,000.

All commissions are computed upon the gross selling price, less points and costs of structural pest control inspection and repairs, if any. Rule 604.

2. **Listing Agreement:** A copy of the proposed listing agreement should be attached to the petition for approval of the agreement. The agreement should provide that in the event the personal representative produces the buyer, the broker will not receive a commission. Commissions are allowed in the event of an overbid in open court. Rule 605.

3. **Sale of Bequeathed Property:** Ten days notice of the hearing must be given to the person to whom it is bequeathed, or his consent must be filed.

SAN BENITO COUNTY

There are no specific local rules on sales.

SAN BERNARDINO COUNTY

1. **Sale of Bequeathed Property:** A sale of specifically bequeathed real or personal property ordinarily will not be confirmed un-

less the written consent of the person to whom it is bequeathed is filed with the petition for confirmation. Rule 804.

2. **Condominiums, Community or Cooperative Apartments:** A condominium is an interest in real property and must be sold as such. A community or cooperative apartment is personal property and must be sold as such. However, the overbid and brokers' commissions on such assets will be computed on the same basis as in real property. The prospective purchaser of a cooperative apartment should obtain acceptance of the Board of Directors before seeking court confirmation. Rule 805.

3. **Sales of Real and Personal Property as a Unit:** When real and personal property are sold as a unit, the report of sale and petition for order confirming sale should clearly set forth the reasons that such sale is in the best interests of the estate. Sales of furniture with dwelling houses, water stocks with lands served thereby, and similar transactions require no detailed explanation. Sales of unrelated real and personal property should, however, be explained in detail. Rule 806.

4. **Mobile Homes:** The court may approve sales of mobile homes as depreciating property. The petition must set forth the efforts to expose the property to the market. Rule 812.

5. **Broker's Commission:** On sales subject to court confirmation, the court will not allow a commission in excess of 6% unless justified by special circumstances. Rule 821(c).

6. **Independent Administration:** Under the IAEA, the personal representative has authority to sell without court confirmation;

however, advice of such sale should be given. Rule 822.

7. Court Confirmation of Private Sales:

a. Cash Deposit to Accompany Bid: The bidder must submit a minimum of 10% of the amount bid. However, exception may be made under special circumstances, for example when the sale is FHA or VA financed. Rule 823(a).

b. Junior Deeds of Trust: The court will approve the taking of a promissory note secured by a junior deed of trust upon a showing that it serves the best interests of the estate. This may require a showing of efforts that were made to sell for cash or a showing of knowledge on the part of the heirs and their lack of objection to acceptance of a junior deed of trust. Rule 823(b).

c. Vesting of Title: The petition for confirmation must set forth the vesting of title in the buyer. The court will not confirm a sale to a "nominee." Rule 823(c).

d. Hearing on Return of Sale and Overbids: Counsel should send notice to the original purchaser or his agent of the time and place of hearing. Rule 823(d).

e. Credit Overbids: The personal representative or counsel should be prepared to inform the court as to the acceptability of credit overbids. Rule 823(e).

f. Ernest Money Deposit by Increased Bidder: When a sale is confirmed to an overbidder, the overbidder, at the request of the personal representative, must submit at the time of the hearing cash or a certified or cashier's check for 10% of the initial overbid.

The personal representative should notify all known anticipated overbidders of this requirement. Rule 823(f).

g. **Overbid Form:** The personal representative or counsel may obtain from the court clerk a form to be completed on the overbid. This form is to be returned to the clerk before the order confirming the sale will be signed. Rule 823(g).

SAN DIEGO COUNTY

1. **Vesting of Title:** The court will not confirm a sale to a "nominee," only to the actual buyer. Rule 4.77.

2. **Listing Agreement:** A specific percentage for comission will not be approved by the court as part of the exclusive listing agreement. Rule 4.79.

3. **Broker's Commission:** A reasonable broker's commission will be determined by the court at the time of confirmation. The court takes current community practices and standards into consideration in making a determination. The court will also inquire into the broker's services in fixing the commission. Rule 4.79.

4. **When Buyer Assumes Encumbrance:** A sale will not ordinarily be confirmed where the buyer assumes or takes subject to an existing encumbrance if the estate is subject to a contingent liability. The report of sale and petition for order confirming sale should set forth the facts pertinent to such assumption agreement. Rule 4.80.

5. Sale of Bequeathed Property: On a sale of specifically bequeathed real or personal property, consent of the person to whom it is bequeathed must be filed with the court. Rule 4.81.

6. Mobile Homes: The court will approve sales of mobile homes as depreciating property. The petition for approval must set forth the efforts to expose the property to the market. Rule 4.83.

7. Sales of Property Will Not Be Confirmed in the Absence of Attorney for the Estate: The court will not proceed with the confirmation of the sale in the absence of the attorney of record except in those cases where the administrator, executor, guardian or conservator is *in propria persona* (acting without an attorney), and in those cases, the personal representative must appear. Rule 4.85.

8. Memorandum of Sale for Use by the Court: At the hearing for a sale of real property the attorney shall provide the court with a memorandum containing the following information:

- Description (insert legal description; if lengthy, use portion of description and refer to notice of sale or petition for complete description).
- Improvements: (type, if any).
- Commonly known as: (address).
- Sold for: ($).
- Terms: (set forth all essential terms).
- Minimum overbid: ($).
- Broker's commission: ($).

- Bond: (waived; additional $ required). Rule 4.86.

9. Increased Bid Form: When there is a successful overbid in open court, an "Increased Bid in Open Court" form must be filled out and signed by the overbidder. Rule 4.88.

10. Allowance of Commissions: When a sale is confirmed upon an overbid and a real estate commission is involved, it shall be the duty of the attorney for the estate to compute the commission and any allocation thereof between brokers, and to report the same to the court for its approval. Rule 4.89.

SAN FRANCISCO COUNTY

1. Exclusive Listings:

    a. In General: The personal representative has authority if acting under the IAEA to enter into an exclusive agreement without prior court approval. At the confirmation hearing, the court will determine the commission (without regard to the terms of the exclusive agreement) and the allocation of it between the selling broker and the broker holding the exclusive. Rule 802(a).

    b. Order: The order for the exclusive listing must provide that if the broker with the exclusive listing does not submit the accepted offer, the commission, if any, to the listing broker will be determined by the court at the time of confirmation of sale. Rule 802(b).

2. Commissions on Personal Property Sales: Commissions will be allowed only to individuals holding a broker's license authorizing them to deal in the type of property involved. A commission will be allowed on the original bid only when the comission is requested in the petition for confirmation of sale. When there is an overbid in court, a commission may be allowed to the successful broker, and, if the original bid was subject to a commission, apportionment between the brokers will be made according to the same rules as prescribed for real estate sales. The amount of the commission is within the court's discretion and will not ordinarily exceed a total of 5% of the sale price. Rule 8.05(b).

3. **Condominiums:** A condominium is an interest in real property and must be sold as such, unless it is held as a limited partnership. Rule 8.07.

4. **Community or Cooperative Apartment:** A community or cooperative apartment is personal property and sold as personal property. Rule 8.07.

a. **Overbid:** Overbids are computed on the same basis as sales in real property.

b. **Broker's Commission:** Broker's commission is allowed on the same basis as in sales of real property.

c. **Acceptance of Board of Directors:** The prospective buyer should obtain acceptance of a Board of Directors of a community or cooperative apartment before petitioning the court for confirmation of sale. Rule 8.07

5. **Return of Private Sale:**

a. **Market Exposure of Property:** If the court finds out that the personal representative has denied bona fide prospective buyers or their brokers a reasonable opportunity to inspect the property, the returned sale will not be confirmed, and the sale will be continued to allow inspection. Rule 8.09(b).

b. **Second Deeds of Trust:** The court will approve the taking of a promissory note secured by a junior deed of trust upon a showing that it serves the best interests of the estate. Rule 8.09(c).

c. **Ernest Money Deposit by Increase Bidder:** When a sale is confirmed to an overbidder, the overbidder, at the request of the personal representative, must submit at the time of the hearing a certified or cashier's check for 10% of the overbid amount, but not to exceed the amount of the cash down payment. Rule 8.09(f.)

d. **Overbid Form:** The courtroom clerk will give the attorney for the personal representative a form to be completed and returned to the clerk before the end of the morning's probate hearings. The form must be signed by the successful overbidder. Rule 8.09(g).

6. **Broker's Commission on Real Property:**

a. **Improved Property:** The court will ordinarily allow a broker's commission not to exceed:

6% of the first $100,000
5% of the next   50,000
2 1/2% of the balance of the sales price.

The parties may agree to a lesser percentage. Rule 8.10a.

b. Unimproved Property: The court will ordinarily allow a broker's commission not to exceed:

10% of the first $20,000
8% of the next $30,000
5% of the balance of the sale price.

In the court's discretion, a flat 10% may be allowed. The court will determine what is unimproved property. Rule 8.10(b).

c. Commission Rates at Property Situs Will Apply: If the property is located in another county, San Francisco County's commission schedule will apply, unless that county's schedule would allow a larger commission. Rule 8.10(d).

d. Commissions in Excess of Schedule: A commission in excess of the normal schedule will be allowed only if it is reasonable in the court's opinion. Whenever possible, the written agreement of the beneficiaries to the excess commission should be obtained. Rule 8.10(e).

e. Broker Bidding for His or Her Own Account: A broker bidding for his or her own account is not entitled to receive or share in a commission. Rule 8.10(f).

7. Broker's Commissions in Overbid Situations: (Rule 8.11).

a. Only Original Bidder Represented by Broker: The original broker is allowed a full commission on the original bid.

b. Both Bidders Represented by Broker: The original broker will receive one-half the commission on the original bid (if the commission agreed on is less than the commission schedule, the original broker is bound by the agreement); the broker representing the successful overbidder receives the remaining one-half commission on the original bid, which in the court's discretion may be based either on the agreement or the commission schedule, plus the full commission on the amount in excess of the original bid based on the commission schedule. The Probate Code limits the commission of the broker for the successful overbidder to half the amount of the difference between the original bid and successful overbid.

c. Only Overbidder Represented by Broker: The broker's commission may not exceed one-half the difference between the original bid and the successful overbid. Within this limit, the court will allow one-half the normal commission on the original bid and a full commission on the overbid.

d. Original Bidder as Overbidder: Once the original bid has been overbid, the original bidder may elect to be represented by a broker in further bidding.

SAN JOAQUIN COUNTY

1. Sale or Encumbrance of Specifically Bequeathed Property: No specifically bequeathed real property shall be encumbered or offered for sale unless first approved by the court after not less than seven days notice to the person to whom it is bequeathed, or unless the consent of the person is on file. Rule 4-601.

2. Shortening Publication Time for Private Sales of Personal or Real Property: When a court order is obtained shortening the time of publication which would otherwise be required for a sale, care should be taken to include a provision similarly shortening the time for posting. Rule 4-607.

3. Broker's Commission: Upon the confirmation of the sale of real property, a broker's commission in excess of 6% of the gross sales price will not be allowed unless otherwise approved by the court. Rule 4-608.

SAN LUIS OBISPO COUNTY

There are no specific local rules on sales.

SAN MATEO COUNTY

1. Exclusive Listings for Sale of Real Property: A personal representative acting under IAEA has authority to enter into an exclusive agreement to sell without prior court approval. The commission and the allocation between brokers will be determined by the court at the hearing on confirmation (without regard to the terms of the exclusive agreement). Rule 440.

2. Sales of Personal Property:

    a. Necessity for Appraisal: Before the court will approve a sale of personal property, the property must be appraised. Rule 442(a).

    b. Commissions: The commission will ordinarily not exceed 5% and is within the court's discretion. A sales commission will only be allowed if the individual is licensed for that type of sale. The commission must be requested in the report of sale and petition for order confirming sale. A commission may be allowed to the broker for a successful overbidder. Apportionment will be made according to rules governing real estate sales. Rule 442(b).

3. **Condominiums, Community or Cooperative Apartments:** A condominium is an interest in real property and must be sold as such, unless it is held as a limited partnership. A community or cooperative apartment is personal property and must be sold as such. However, the overbid and brokers' commissions will be allowed on the same basis as in sales of real property. The prospective purchaser of a cooperative apartment should obtain acceptance of the Board of Directors before seeking court confirmation. Rule 444.

4. **Publication of Notice of Intention to Sell Real Property:** The notice should state if an exclusive listing has been given and if the property is being sold subject to an encumbrance. Rule 445(b).

5. **Market Exposure of Property:** If the court finds out that the personal representative has denied bona fide prospective buyers or their brokers a reasonable opportunity to inspect the property, the returned sale will not be confirmed, and the sale will be continued to allow inspection. Rule 446(b).

6. **Second Deeds of Trust:** The court will approve the taking of a promissory note secured by a junior deed of trust upon a showing that it serves the best interests of the estate. Rule 442(c).

7. Ernest Money Deposit by Bidder: The bid must be accompanied by a minimum deposit of 10% of the amount bid in cash or its equivalent. The overbidder must submit 10% of his overbid in cash or its equivalent at the time of the hearing. Rule 446(f).

8. Overbid Form: The courtroom clerk will give the attorney for the representative a form. The form must be completed and signed by the overbidder and returned to the clerk before the end of that morning's probate hearings. Rule 446(g).

9. Broker's Commission on Real Property:

a. Improved Property: The court will ordinarily allow a broker's commission not to exceed:

6% of the first $100,000
5% of the next   50,000
2 1/2% of the balance of the sale
        price

Rule 447(a).

b. Unimproved Property: The court will ordinarily allow a broker's commission not to exceed:

10% of the first $20,000
8% of the next $30,000
5% of the balance of the sale
        price.

The court, in its discretion, may allow a flat 10%. The court will determine what is "unimproved" real property. Rule 447(b).

c. Commission Rates at Property Situs Will Apply: If the property is located in another county, San Mateo County's commission schedule will apply, unless that county's schedule would allow a larger commission. Rule 447(d).

d. **Broker Bidding for Own Account:** A broker bidding for his or her own account is not entitled to receive or share in a commission. Rule 447(e).

10. **Broker's Commission in Overbid Situations:** (Rule 448)

a. **Only Original Bidder Represented by Broker:** The original broker is allowed a full commission on the amount of the original bid.

b. **Overbidder Represented by Broker:** Overbidder's broker receives a full commission on the overbid, reduced by one-half the commission on the original bid, which latter commission goes to the broker for the original bidder, if any. This latter commission will be split equally with any listing broker involved. Overbidder's commission is limited to half the difference between the successful overbid and the original bid.

c. **Original Bidder as Overbidder:** Once the original bid has been overbid, the original bidder may elect to be represented by a broker in further bidding.

SANTA BARBARA COUNTY

1. **Broker's Commission:** The court will not approve a real estate commission in excess of 6% except in unusual cases where a larger commission is justified because of exceptional circumstances. Rule F.2.

2. **Description:** The petition to confirm sale of real property shall, in addition to the

legal description, contain the street address or other familiar designation of property. Rule F.3.

3. Appearance by Attorney: In petitions for confirmation of sale of real property and for sale of personal property where bidding is authorized, the court ordinarily will not proceed with confirmation of the sale in the absence of the attorney of record. Rule F.4.

4. Sale of Personal Property: Sales of personal property will not be approved or confirmed unless the property has been appraised. Rule F.5.

5. Approval of Overbid: If the sale returned for confirmation is upon credit, a higher bid, whether or on the same or additional credit terms, shall not be approved unless the personal representative, or the personal representative's attorney, informs the court that the overbid is acceptable. Rule F.7.

SANTA CLARA COUNTY

1. Notice of Sale: If the property to be sold is subject to an encumbrance, the published notice should so state. It is advisable that the published notice call for "cash or such credit terms and conditions as the Court may approve."

On filing an appropriate affidavit or declaration, the court may sign an order shortening time for publication to five days with sale on the sixth day. The practical effect of this order is that only one publication is necessary. Rule 7.1.

2. Petition for Confirmation of Sale of Real Property:

a. Time for Filing: The petition must be filed within 30 days after the date of acceptance of a contract. Note that the property is initially sold by the personal representative and then returned to the court for confirmation. Rule 7.2.1.

b. Deed of Trust: Upon an appropriate showing by the personal representative, the court may approve a sale where part of the consideration is to be secured by a deed of trust of which the personal representative is the beneficiary. Rule 7.2.2.

c. Hearing to Confirm Sale: The attorney for the personal representative, or the representative if acting as his or her own attorney, must be present or the hearing will be continued. Rule 7.2.3.

d. Notice to Purchaser: Notice of the time and place of hearing shall be given to the original purchaser or his or her agent. Rule 7.2.4.

e. Sale Subject to Encumbrance: Sale of real property will not ordinarily be confirmed if the purchaser assumes or takes subject to an existing encumbrance, if as a result the estate remains subject to a contingent liability. The petition shall set forth the pertinent facts. Rule 7.2.5.

SANTA CRUZ COUNTY

1. Broker's Commission: A broker who purchases real property is not entitled to a commission, even if he or she is the listing broker. Rule 412.

SHASTA COUNTY

1. Sale or Encumbrance of Specifically Bequeathed Property: No specifically bequeathed real or personal property shall be encumbered or offered for sale unless first approved by the court on seven court days notice to the person to whom it was bequeathed. Rule 12.14, Uniform Rules of Third District Superior Courts.

SIERRA COUNTY

1. Sale or Encumbrance of Specifically Bequeathed Property: No specifically bequeathed real or personal property shall be encumbered or offered for sale unless first approved by the court on seven court days notice to the person to whom it was bequeathed. Rule 12.14, Uniform Rules of Third District Superior Courts.

SISKIYOU COUNTY

1. Sale or Encumbrance of Specifically Bequeathed Property: No specifically bequeathed real or personal property shall be encumbered or offered for sale unless first approved by the court on seven court days notice to the person to whom it was bequeathed. Rule

12.14, Uniform Rules of Third District Superior Courts.

SOLANO COUNTY

1. **Cash Deposit:** A minimum deposit of 10% of the purchase price, unless the loan proceeds exceed 90% of the purchase price, must be deposited in escrow 10 days prior to the confirmation of sale hearing and written verification filed five days prior to the hearing. Rule 7.26.

2. **Second Deeds of Trust:** The court will approve the taking of a promissory note secured by a second deed of trust upon a showing that it serves the best interests of the estate. Rule 7.27.

3. **Ernest Money Deposit by Overbidder:** When a sale is confirmed to an overbidder, the overbidder must submit at the time of the hearing a certified or cashier's check for 10% of the bid. Rule 7.28.

4. **Increased Bid Forms:** In the event of a successful overbid, the successful bidder must sign an "Increased Bid in Open Court" form and file it with the court. Rule 7.31.

5. **Conditional Sales of Real Property:** The Court will ordinarily not approve a sale of real property which is conditioned upon the occurrence of a subsequent event (such as a change in zoning or obtaining approval from an environmental control board). However, if unusual and extraordinary circumstances exist and the necessity and advantage to the estate

are set forth in detail, the court may approve such a sale. Rule 7.32.

6. **Broker's Commission:** (Rule 7.33)

a. **Improved Real Property:** Ordinarily not to exceed 6% of the sales price.

b. **Unimproved Real Property:** Ordinarily not to exceed:

10% of the first $20,000
8% of the next   30,000
5 % of the balance.

SONOMA COUNTY

1. **Overbids:** When there is a successful overbid, the successful bidder must sign an "Increased Bid in Open Court" form and file it with the court. Rule 9.7(a).

2. **Disputes Between Agents or Brokers Regarding Compensation:** Should a dispute arise between agents or brokers seeking compensation, there shall be a separate evidentiary hearing to resolve the dispute. The sale of real property may be confirmed at the hearing on the sale and need not be delayed by virtue of the dispute. Rule 9.7(b).

STANISLAUS COUNTY

1. **Sale of Bequeathed Property:** No specifically bequeathed real property shall be encumbered or offered for sale unless first approved by the court after not less than ten days notice to the person to whom it is bequeathed, or unless the consent of the person is on file. Rule 801.

2. Exclusive Listing: The court takes the position that in almost all cases it is to the advantage of the estate to have its real property placed on multiple listing and exposed to the sales efforts of as many brokers as possible. In extraordinary cases (for example, sale of an undivided interest, or of real property whose value is very small in comparison to the problems involved), upon proof of sufficient necessity or advantage to the estate, the court may grant the petition for exclusive listing. A copy of the proposed agreement should be attached to the petition. No such agreement shall provide for the payment of a commission to the broker holding the listing in the event of a sale to a buyer produced by the personal representative, although commissions will be allowed in the event of increased bids in open court. Rule 803.

3. Broker's Commission: The court will allow a sales commission not in excess of 6% of the gross sales price unless prior court order was obtained. Rule 807.

4. Deposit to Accompany Overbid in Court: The bid must be accompanied by a minimum of 10% of the bid amount. The successful overbidder must submit at time of the hearing a certified or cashier's check in an amount equal to 10% of the first allowable minimum overbid. Rule 808.

5. Conditional Sales of Real Property: The court will ordinarily not approve a sale of real property which is conditioned upon the occurrence of a subsequent event (such as change in zoning or obtaining approval from an environmental control board). However, if unusual and extraordinary circumstances exist and the necessity and advantage to the estate are set forth in detail the court may approve such a sale. Rule 812.

6. **Sales When Buyer Assumes Encumbrance:** A sale will not ordinarily be confirmed where the buyer assumes an existing encumbrance if the estate is subject to a contingent liability. The report of sale and petition for order confirming sale should state any facts pertinent to the assumption agreement and the contingent liability, if any. Rule 813.

SUTTER COUNTY

1. **Sale or Encumbrance of Specifically Bequeathed Property:** No specifically bequeathed real or personal property shall be encumbered or offered for sale unless first approved by the court on seven court days notice to the person to whom it was bequeathed. Rule 12.14, Uniform Rules of Third District Superior Courts.

TEHAMA COUNTY

1. **Sale or Encumbrance of Specifically Bequeathed Property:** No specifically bequeathed real or personal property shall be encumbered or offered for sale unless first approved by the court on seven court days notice to the person to whom it was bequeathed. Rule 12.14, Uniform Rules of Third District Superior Courts.

TRINITY COUNTY

1. Sale or Encumbrance of Specifically Bequeathed Property: No specifically bequeathed real or personal property shall be encumbered or offered for sale unless first approved by the court on seven court days notice to the person to whom it was bequeathed. Rule 12.14, Uniform Rules of Third District Superior Courts.

TULARE COUNTY

1. Broker's Commission: Where the sale price is $500 or more, the court will not approve a commission in excess of 6% of the sales price unless it is justified by exceptional circumstances. Rule 5(c).

TUOLUMNE COUNTY

1. Sale or Encumbrance of Specifically Bequeathed Property: No specifically bequeathed real or personal property shall be encumbered or offered for sale unless first approved by the court on seven court days notice to the person to whom it was bequeathed. Rule 12.13.

VENTURA COUNTY

1. Petition for Confirmation of Sale: A petition for confirmation of sale of real property should set forth a brief description of the property; the amount bid; the name of the bidder; appraised value and date thereof; amount of commission payable and to whom; the necessary minimum increase in bid; the amount of bond in force at the time of sale; additional bond, if any, required. If no additional bond is required, or if bond is waived, that fact should be alleged. Rule 11.11(a).

2. **Absence of Counsel:** In a petition for confirmation of sale of real estate and for sale of personal property when bidding is authorized, the court will not proceed with the confirmation of sale in the absence of counsel except in those cases where the administrator, executor, or guardian is present and requests that the sale proceed. Rule 11.11(b).

3. **Broker's Commission:** Upon the confirmation of the sale of real property where the sale price is $500 or more, the court will not allow a broker's commission in excess of 6% unless it is justified by exceptional circumstances. Rule 11.11(c).

YOLO COUNTY

1. **Broker's Commission:**
   a. **Improved Real Property:** 6%.
   b. **Unimproved Real Property:**
      10% on first $20,000
      8% on next $30,000
      5% on amount over $50,000.
Farm property is usually considered unimproved property. Rule 20.1.

2. **Commission to Agent Securing Increased Bid:** In the event of a successful over-

bid, the court will allow the agent for the over-bidder one-half of the authorized commission on the original bid and the full commission on the remainder of the purchase price, if the total commission does not exceed the maximum allowed by the Probate Code (limitation of not more than one-half the difference between the original bid and the successful overbid). Rule 20.2.

YUBA COUNTY

1. **Sale or Encumbrance of Specifically Bequeathed Property:** No specifically bequeathed real or personal property shall be encumbered or offered for sale unless first approved by the court on seven court days notice to the person to whom it was bequeathed. Rule 12.14, Uniform Rules of Third District Superior Courts.

Index